MACMILLAN MASTER GUIDES

A MIDSUMMER NIGHT'S DREAM
BY WILLIAM SHAKESPEARE

MACMILLAN MASTER GUIDES

General Editor: James Gibson

Published:
JANE AUSTEN: **EMMA** Norman Page
ROBERT BOLT: **A MAN FOR ALL SEASONS** Leonard Smith
EMILY BRONTË: **WUTHERING HEIGHTS** Hilda D. Spear
GEOFFREY CHAUCER: **THE PROLOGUE TO THE CANTERBURY TALES** Nigel Thomas and Richard Swan
CHARLES DICKENS: **GREAT EXPECTATIONS** Dennis Butts
GEORGE ELIOT: **SILAS MARNER** Graham Handley
GEORGE ORWELL: **ANIMAL FARM** Jean Armstrong
WILLIAM SHAKESPEARE: **MACBETH** David Elloway
    A MIDSUMMER NIGHT'S DREAM Kenneth Pickering
    ROMEO AND JULIET Helen Morris

Forthcoming:
JANE AUSTEN: **MANSFIELD PARK** Richard Wirdnam
    PRIDE AND PREJUDICE Raymond Wilson
CHARLES DICKENS: **HARD TIMES** Norman Page
GEORGE ELIOT: **MIDDLEMARCH** Graham Handley
T. S. ELIOT: **MURDER IN THE CATHEDRAL** Paul Lapworth
OLIVER GOLDSMITH: **SHE STOOPS TO CONQUER** Paul Ranger
THOMAS HARDY: **FAR FROM THE MADDING CROWD** Colin Temblett-Wood
    TESS OF THE D'URBERVILLES James Gibson
CHRISTOPHER MARLOWE: **DR FAUSTUS** David Male
THE METAPHYSICAL POETS Joan van Emden
WILLIAM SHAKESPEARE: **HAMLET** Jean Brooks
    TWELFTH NIGHT Edward Leeson
    THE WINTER'S TALE Diana Devlin
GEORGE BERNARD SHAW: **ST JOAN** Leonee Ormond
R. B. SHERIDAN: **THE RIVALS** Jeremy Rowe

Also published by Macmillan

MACMILLAN MASTER SERIES

Mastering English Literature R. Gill
Mastering English Language S. H. Burton
Mastering English Grammar S. H. Burton

MACMILLAN MASTER GUIDES
A MIDSUMMER NIGHT'S DREAM
BY WILLIAM SHAKESPEARE

KENNETH PICKERING

MACMILLAN

© Kenneth Pickering 1985

All rights reserved. No reproduction, copy or transmission
of this publication may be made without written permission.

No paragraph of this publication may be reproduced, copied
or transmitted save with written permission or in accordance
with the provisions of the Copyright Act 1956 (as amended).

Any person who does any unauthorised act in relation to
this publication may be liable to criminal prosecution and
civil claims for damages.

First edition 1985
Reprinted 1985

Published by
MACMILLAN EDUCATION LTD
Houndmills, Basingstoke, Hampshire RG21 2XS
and London
Companies and representatives
throughout the world

Typeset in Great Britain by
TEC SET, Sutton, Surrey

Printed in Hong Kong

British Library Cataloguing in Publication Data
Pickering, Kenneth
A midsummer night's dream by William Shakespeare.
— (Macmillan master guides)
1. Shakespeare, William. Midsummer night's dream
I. Title
822.3'3   PR2827
ISBN 0–333–37289–1
ISBN 0–333–39296–5 (export)

CONTENTS

General editor's preface		vi
Acknowledgements		vii
An introduction to the study of Shakespeare's plays		viii
1 William Shakespeare: life and background		1
		4
2 Summaries and critical commentary	2.1 The play	6
	2.2 Origin and sources	6
	2.4 Plot summary	8
	2.5 Scene summaries and critical commentary	10
3 Themes and issues	3.1 Love and marriage	36
	3.2 Discord and concord	38
	3.3 Imagination	38
	3.4 Dreams, illusions and reality	39
4 Techniques	4.1 Characters and characterisation	41
	4.2 The language	48
	4.3 Rhyme and rhythm	50
	4.4 Imagery and mythology	53
	4.5 Music and dance	58
	4.6 *A Midsummer Night's Dream* in the theatre	61
5 Specimen passage and commentary	5.1 Specimen passage	68
	5.2 Commentary	69
6 Critical appraisals	6.1 General criticisms of the play	73
	6.2 Theatre criticisms	75
Revision questions		78
Appendix: Shakespeare's Theatre		80
Further reading		84

GENERAL EDITOR'S PREFACE

The aim of the Macmillan Master Guides is to help you to appreciate the book you are studying by providing information about it and by suggesting ways of reading and thinking about it which will lead to a fuller understanding. The section on the writer's life and background has been designed to illustrate those aspects of the writer's life which have influenced the work, and to place it in its personal and literary context. The summaries and critical commentary are of special importance in that each brief summary of the action is followed by an examination of the significant critical points. The space which might have been given to repetitive explanatory notes has been devoted to a detailed analysis of the kind of passage which might confront you in an examination. Literary criticism is concerned with both the broader aspects of the work being studied and with its detail. The ideas which meet us in reading a great work of literature, and their relevance to us today, are an essential part of our study, and our Guides look at the thought of their subject in some detail. But just as essential is the craft with which the writer has constructed his work of art, and this is considered under several technical headings – characterisation, language, style and stagecraft.

The authors of these Guides are all teachers and writers of wide experience, and they have chosen to write about books they admire and know well in the belief that they can communicate their admiration to you. But you yourself must read and know intimately the book you are studying. No one can do that for you. You should see this book as a lamp-post. Use it to shed light, not to lean against. If you know your text and know what it is saying about life, and how it says it, then you will enjoy it, and there is no better way of passing an examination in literature.

JAMES GIBSON

ACKNOWLEDGEMENTS

I am pleased to acknowledge the help and encouragement of Dr Derek Hyde, Dr James Gibson, Professor Harold Brooks and my sister, Jean Pickering, in the preparation of this book.

K. P.

Cover illustration is *Sketch for the Enchanted Wood: A Midsummer Night's Dream* by N. A. Shifrin, courtesy of the Central Theatre of The Red Army, Moscow. The drawing of the Globe Theatre is by courtesy of Alec Pearson.

NOTE. It is important to use a good modern edition of the play which has the benefits of recent scholarship. The recommended edition to which all references will apply in this guide is *A Midsummer Night's Dream* edited by Norman Saunders in *The Macmillan Shakespeare*. This contains a particularly helpful introduction. The Arden Edition, edited by Professor Harold Brooks, will be found invaluable.

AN INTRODUCTION TO THE STUDY OF SHAKESPEARE'S PLAYS

A play as a work of art exists to the full only when performed. It must hold the audience's attention throughout the performance, and, unlike a novel, it can't be put down and taken up again. It is important to experience the play as if you are seeing it on the stage for the first time, and you should begin by reading it straight through. Shakespeare builds a play in dramatic units which may be divided into smaller subdivisions, or episodes, marked off by exits and entrances and lasting as long as the same actors are on the stage. Study it unit by unit.

The first unit provides the exposition which is designed to put the audience into the picture. In the second unit we see the forward movement of the play as one situation changes into another. The last unit in a tragedy or a tragical play will bring the catastrophe and in comedy – and some of the history plays – an unravelling of the complications, what is called a *dénouement*.

The onward movement of the play from start to finish is its progressive structure. We see the chain of cause and effect (the plot) and the progressive revelation and development of character. The people, their characters and their motives drive the plot forward in a series of scenes which are carefully planned to give variety of pace and excitement. We notice fast-moving and slower-moving episodes, tension mounting and slackening, and alternate fear and hope for the characters we favour. Full-stage scenes, such as stately councils and processions or turbulent mobs, contrast with scenes of small groups or even single speakers. Each of the scenes presents a deed or event which changes the situation. In performance, entrances and exits and stage actions are physical facts, with more impact than on the page. That impact Shakespeare relied upon, and we must restore it by an effort of the imagination.

Shakespeare's language is just as diverse. Quickfire dialogue is followed by long speeches, and verse changes to prose. There is a wide range of speech – formal, colloquial, dialect, 'Mummerset' and the broken English of foreigners, for example. Songs, instrumental music, and the noise of battle, revelry and tempest, all extend the range of dramatic expression. The dramatic use of language is enhanced by skilful stagecraft, by costumes, by properties such as beds, swords and Yorick's skull, by such stage business as kneeling, embracing and giving money, and by use of such features of the stage structure as the balcony and the trapdoor.

By these means Shakespeare's people are brought vividly to life and cleverly individualised. But though they have much to tell us about human nature, we must never forget that they are characters in a play, not in real life. And remember, they exist to enact the play, not the play to portray *them*.

Shakespeare groups his characters so that they form a pattern, and it is useful to draw a diagram showing this. Sometimes a linking character has dealings with each group. The pattern of persons belongs to the symmetric structure of the play, and its dramatic unity is reinforced and enriched by a pattern of resemblances and contrasts; for instance, between characters, scenes, recurrent kinds of imagery, and words. It is not enough just to notice a feature that belongs to the symmetric structure, you should ask what its relevance is to the play as a whole and to the play's ideas.

These ideas and the dramatising of them in a central theme, or several related to each other, are a principal source of the dramatic unity. In order to see what themes are present and important, look, as before, for pattern. Observe the place in it of the leading character. In tragedy this will be the protagonist, in comedy heroes and heroines, together with those in conflict or contrast with them. In *I Henry IV*, Prince Hal is being educated for kingship and has a correct estimate of honour, while Falstaff despises honour, and Hotspur makes an idol of it. Pick out the episodes of great intensity as, for example, in *King Lear* where the theme of spiritual blindness is objectified in the blinding of Gloucester, and, similarly, note the emphases given by dramatic poetry as in Prospero's 'Our revels now are ended. . .' or unforgettable utterances such as Lear's 'Is there any cause in Nature that makes these hard hearts?' Striking stage-pictures such as that of Hamlet behind the King at prayer will point to leading themes, as will all the parallels and recurrences, including those of phrase and imagery. See whether, in the play you are studying, themes known to be favourites with Shakespeare are prominent, themes such as those of order and disorder, relationships disrupted by mistakes about identity, and appearance and reality. The latter were bound to fascinate Shakespeare whose theatrical art worked by means of illusions which pointed beyond the surface of actual life to underlying truths. In looking at themes beware of attempts to make the play fit some orthodoxy a critic believes in – Freudian perhaps, or Marxist, or dogmatic Christian theology – and remember that its ideas, though they often have a bearing on ours, are Elizabethan.

Some of Shakespeare's greatness lies in the good parts he wrote for the actors. In his demands upon them, and the opportunities he provided, he bore their professional skills in mind and made use of their physical prowess, relished by a public accustomed to judge fencing and wrestling as expertly as we today judge football and tennis. As a member of the professional group of players called the Chamberlain's Men he knew each actor he was writing for. To play his women he had highly-trained boys. As paired heroines they were often contrasted, short with tall, for example, or one vivacious and enterprising, the other more conventionally feminine.

Richard Burbage, the company's leading man, was famous as a great tragic actor, and he took leading roles in seven of Shakespeare's *tragedies*. Though each of the seven has its own distinctiveness, we shall find at the centre of all of them a tragic protagonist possessing tragic greatness, not just one 'tragic flaw' but a tragic vulnerability. He will have a character which makes him unfit to cope with the tragic situations confronting him, so that his tragic errors bring down upon him tragic suffering and finally a tragic catastrophe. Normally, both the suffering and the catastrophe are far worse than he can be said to deserve, and others are engulfed in them who deserve such a fate less or not at all. Tragic terror is aroused in us because, though exceptional, he is sufficiently near to normal humankind for his fate to remind us of what can happen to human beings like ourselves, and because we see in it a combination of inexorable law and painful mystery. We recognise the principle of cause and effect where in a tragic world errors return upon those who make them, but we are also aware of the tragic disproportion between cause and effect. In a tragic world you may kick a stone and start an avalanche which will destroy you and others with you. Tragic pity is aroused in us by this disproportionate suffering, and also by all the kinds of suffering undergone by every character who has won our imaginative sympathy. Imaginative sympathy is wider than moral approval, and is felt even if suffering does seem a just and logical outcome. In addition to pity and terror we have a sense of tragic waste because catastrophe has affected so much that was great and fine. Yet we feel also a tragic exaltation. To our grief the men and women who represented those values have been destroyed, but the values themselves have been shown not to depend upon success, nor upon immunity from the worse of tragic suffering and disaster.

Comedies have been of two main kinds, or cross-bred from the two. In critical comedies the governing aim is to bring out the absurdity or irrationality of follies and abuses, and make us laugh at them. Shakespeare's comedies often do this, but most of them belong primarily to the other kind – romantic comedy. Part of the romantic appeal is to our liking for suspense; they are dramas of averted threat, beginning in trouble and ending in joy. They appeal to the romantic senses of adventure and of wonder, and to complain that they are improbable is silly because the improbability, the marvellousness, is part of the pleasure. They dramatise stories of romantic love, accompanied by love doctrine – ideas and ideals of love. But they are plays in two tones, they are comic as well as romantic. There is often something to laugh at even in the love stories of the nobility and gentry, and just as there is high comedy in such incidents as the cross-purposes of the young Athenians in the wood, and Rosalind as 'Ganymede' teasing Orlando, there is always broad comedy for characters of lower rank. Even where one of the sub-plots has no effect on the main plot, it may take up a topic from it and present it in a more comic way.

What is there in the play to make us laugh or smile? We can distinguish many kinds of comedy it may employ. *Language* can amuse by its wit, or by absurdity, as in Bottom's malapropisms. Feste's nonsense-phrases, so fatuously admired by Sir Andrew, are deliberate, while his catechising of Olivia is clown-routine. Ass-headed Bottom embraced by the Fairy Queen is a *comic spectacle* combining costume and stage-business. His wanting to play every part is *comedy of character*. Phebe disdaining Silvius and in love with 'Ganymede', or Malvolio treating Olivia as though she had written him a love-letter is *comedy of situation*; the situation is laughably different from what Phebe or Malvolio supposes. A comic let-down or anticlimax can be devastating, as we see when Aragon, sure that he deserves Portia, chooses the silver casket only to find the portrait not of her but of a 'blinking idiot'. By *slapstick*, *caricature* or sheer *ridiculousness of situation*, comedy can be exaggerated into farce, which Shakespeare knows how to use on occasion. At the opposite extreme, before he averts the threat, he can carry it to the brink of tragedy, but always under control.

Dramatic irony is the result of a character or the audience anticipating an outcome which, comically or tragically, turns out very differently. Sometimes *we* foresee that it will. The speaker never foresees how ironical, looking back, the words or expectations will appear. When she says, 'A little water clears us of this deed' Lady Macbeth has no prevision of her sleep-walking words, 'Will these hands ne'er be clean?' There is irony in the way in which in all Shakespeare's tragic plays except *Richard II* comedy is found in the very heart of the tragedy. The Porter scene in *Macbeth* comes straight after Duncan's murder. In *Hamlet* and *Antony and Cleopatra* comic episodes lead into the catastrophe: the rustic Countryman brings Cleopatra the means of death, and the satirised Osric departs with Hamlet's assent to the fatal fencing match. The Porter, the Countryman and Osric are not mere 'comic relief', they contrast with the tragedy in a way that adds something to it, and affects our response.

A sense of the comic and the tragic is common ground between Shakespeare and his audience. Understandings shared with the audience are necessary to all drama. They include conventions, i.e. assumptions, contrary to what factual realism would demand, which the audience silently agrees to accept. It is, after all, by a convention, what Coleridge called a 'willing suspension of disbelief', that an actor is accepted as Hamlet. We should let a play teach us the conventions it depends on. Shakespeare's conventions allow him to take a good many liberties, and he never troubles about inconsistencies that wouldn't trouble an audience. What matters to the dramatist is the effect he creates. So long as we are responding as he would wish, Shakespeare would not care whether we could say by what means he has made us do so. But to appreciate his skill, and get a fuller understanding of his play, we have to distinguish these means, and find terms to describe them.

If you approach the Shakespeare play you are studying bearing in mind what is said to you here, then you will respond to it more fully than before. Yet like all works of artistic genius, Shakespeare's can only be analysed so far. His drama and its poetry will always have about them something 'which into words no critic can digest'.

HAROLD BROOKS

1 WILLIAM SHAKESPEARE: LIFE AND BACKGROUND

We know comparatively little about the life and career of Shakespeare and what we do know has to be pieced together from fragments of evidence. He spent much of his life involved in the theatre which (though not for the same reason) was probably as precarious an existence in Elizabethan times as it is today, and actors enjoyed little social standing and left few records. Playwrights and actors were too preoccupied with rehearsing, performing and preparing scripts for the next show to be over-conerned with the interest of posterity but such evidence as we have suggests that William Shakespeare was an unusually shrewd businessman and a very popular dramatist in his own lifetime.

He was born in Stratford-upon-Avon, Warwickshire, and baptised on 26th April, 1564. At the time of his birth Shakespeare's father, John, was a prosperous glover who four years later became town Bailiff, but after this he gradually appears to have got into financial difficulties and it was left to William to restore the family fortunes from his success in the theatre. William was probably educated at Stratford Grammar School, acquiring what the playwright Ben Jonson described as Shakespeare's 'small Latin'; it was, however, enough to enable him to read the poet Ovid and the dramatists Terence, Plautus and Seneca in the original. There is at least one reliable report that Shakespeare worked as a schoolmaster for a time and we can be certain of his marriage, in 1582, to Anne Hathaway from neighbouring Shottery and of the birth of their children, Susanna (baptised 26th May, 1583) and the twins Judith and Hamnet (baptised 2nd February, 1585).

At some stage, probably following the birth of his children, Shakespeare decided to become an actor; we do not know precisely why or when, but there are records that between December 1586 and December 1587 five companies of actors visited Stratford and he may well have been recruited by one of them.

By 1592 Shakespeare had made his mark in London with three successful history plays: the First, Second and Third parts of *Henry VI* and he soon became a shareholder in a company of actors known as the Chamberlain's Men who established themselves at the 'Theatre', a playhouse owned by James Burbage in the northern suburbs of London. From his lodgings in Bishopsgate Shakespeare was able to work with the leading actors of his day including Will Kempe, a brilliant 'clown' and Richard Burbage, a fine tragedian, and many of the roles in his plays were, no doubt, written to suit their particular talents.

In the late sixteenth and early seventeenth century performing and creative artists were held in rather low esteem and in order to gain recognition relied heavily on support from noble patrons or from the Court itself; Shakespeare was no exception. In 1595 he was among members of the Chamberlain's Men who received a fee for two performances at Court; his play *The Comedy of Errors* was chosen for revival by the lawyers of Gray's Inn and it is highly probable that *A Midsummer Night's Dream* was commissioned in 1596 for the celebrations at the wedding of the daughter of Sir George Carey, the Chamberlain's Men's patron. Similarly, *The Merry Wives of Windsor* was probably performed at the Garter Feast in 1597 when Sir George was made a Knight of the Order.

The years 1593 and 1594 brought particular problems to the Chamberlain's Men because the plague forced the closure of the theatre for substantial periods. However, the enterprising Shakespeare showed remarkable adaptability and found a new patron in the youthful Earl of Southampton for whom he wrote and published two narrative poems, *Venus and Adonis* (1593) and *The Rape of Lucrece* (1594), and we think that Southampton enabled *Love's Labour's Lost* to have private first performances. It was in the difficult years between 1594 and 1599 that Shakespeare also completed *The Merchant of Venice, Romeo and Juliet, As You Like It, Much Ado About Nothing, Richard II*, the two parts of *Henry IV, Henry V* and, probably, *Twelfth Night*.

This remarkable achievement was only surpassed by Shakespeare's response to a new set of circumstances. In 1599 the Theatre was dismantled and its timbers ferried across the Thames to build the Globe on Bankside. Shakespeare was a 'householder' or part landlord and against a background of growing political tension the Chamberlain's Men were bribed to revive *Richard II* with its deposition scene as a comment on the Earl of Essex's political ambitions which led him to return to England against the Queen's wishes and to his rebellion and execution in 1601. Southampton, Shakespeare's patron and one of the supporters of Essex, was imprisoned and though the actors were not punished they had come perilously near to the power struggle.

When Elizabeth died in 1603 the Chamberlain's Men became the King's

Men with the status of minor Court officials. *Macbeth* (1606) does honour to King James's union of the English and Scottish crowns, and the other great tragedies – *Othello*, *King Lear* and *Hamlet* – and the political Roman plays – *Julius Caesar*, *Coriolanus* and *Antony and Cleopatra* – all belong to Shakespeare's years at the Globe, together with what are sometimes called the 'problem' plays – *Troilus and Cressida*, *All's Well That Ends Well* and *Measure for Measure*. We know few details of Shakespeare's personal life during this period except that he was already making substantial investments in Stratford as a preparation for his retirement from London. The King's Men purchased a new *indoor* theatre, the Blackfriars in 1608, and Shakespeare's final phase as a playwright seems to reflect the changed theatrical conditions for which he was writing. *Pericles*, *Cymbeline*, *The Winter's Tale* and *The Tempest* all benefit from production in a more intimate theatre space although it is not certain that these plays were exclusively written for the Blackfriars; the Globe continued in use until it was destroyed by fire.

By 1612, though he continued to visit London, Shakespeare seems to have had no residence there and apart from collaborating with John Fletcher on *Henry VIII* (1613) and *The Two Noble Kinsmen* (probably 1613) he wrote no further plays. He died in Stratford in 1616 and left a will which still exists.

Though our sketchy knowledge of Shakespeare's life is tantalising, the essential fact to grasp in studying his plays is that he was basically a working play*wright*, a maker of plays, who responded to the pressure, changing tastes and conditions of the theatre of his day and it is to the nature of that theatre that we turn our attention in an Appendix.

2 SUMMARIES AND CRITICAL COMMENTARY

2.1 THE PLAY

Ever since its first performances *A Midsummer Night's Dream* has been one of Shakespeare's most popular plays. In addition to countless productions by professional and amateur theatre companies it has been adapted to make a ballet and at least two operas, made into a film and a television presentation and attracted leading performers, directors and composers to work on its text. In modern times the play has, if anything, become even more popular: it is one of the very few plays by any author to have been in the repertoire of both the National Theatre and The Royal Shakespeare Company at the same time, and Peter Brook's production at Stratford in 1970 is still remembered as something of a landmark in the interpretation of Shakespeare for the modern theatre.

There are a number of reasons why *A Midsummer Night's Dream* is such a perennial favourite with theatre audiences: many critics and directors would argue that it is, quite simply, Shakespeare's best comedy, but unless we have an intimate knowledge of *all* Shakespeare's comedies we are in no position to defend or attack that view. We can, however, list a number of reasons for the play's appeal and others should emerge during the course of our study.

Firstly, it is a very funny play; any good production should have the audience in fits of laughter for a considerable proportion of the action and it is no coincidence that it is the one Shakespeare play in which such popular entertainers as the Beatles and Frankie Howerd have performed.

Secondly, *A Midsummer Night's Dream* offers very good performance opportunities to a large cast, including some excellent parts for several women – though we must remember that these would have been played by boys in Shakespeare's day. His plays often contain a small number of central characters with very large parts to learn but *A Midsummer Night's*

Dream makes a relatively even spread of demands on its cast; there is no obvious 'star' part but many very rewarding roles. It is, therefore, more enjoyable for everyone to rehearse and is less difficult to present.

Thirdly, the play is composed of *two* particular blends which have always created popular entertainment. The first of these is a blend of fantasy and reality; at one moment we are in a dream world of spirits and incredible events and in the next instant we recognise ourselves and our human weakness. The action of the play is never so removed from the real world as to be unacceptable and yet it feeds and works upon our imaginations so that we enter new worlds. Some of the effect of the play in performance is the result of its *other* successful blend: that of music, dance and language. In terms of box office success in the modern theatre 'musicals' have broken all records and although it would be a mistake to describe *A Midsummer Night's Dream* as a stage musical it does contain some of the elements that have accounted for the phenomenal popularity of that genre.

One of the great problems of this particular play is that it is so comparatively well known that many people *think* they understand and appreciate it when in fact they have an entirely superficial knowledge of it. This is partly because the play contains a number of fairy characters and is, therefore, quite mistakenly felt to be suitable only for young children. Many students grow up with a memory of characters like Puck, Titania or Bottom in a play to which they were introduced far too young and they therefore have difficulty in considering it as a serious, though not solemn, work of art. In fact, *A Midsummer Night's Dream* deals with a number of very *adult* issues which are as central to our experience and as relevant to the moment as they were when the play was first written. Questions concerning sexual attraction and love, the interference of parents in love affairs and the nature of marriage dominate much of the action but other problems such as the difference between illusion and reality, the results of jealousy and antagonism, the value of imagination and the purpose of drama and entertainment itself are all presented and examined in this fascinating play. Although we may laugh at their antics, the passions and ambitions which drive the characters of the play are as urgent and real as ours and however comical they may seem to us, the events of that midsummer night had all the makings of a nightmare for many of those involved in its complex drama. We must remember too that for the original audiences for whom the play was written, the belief in supernatural beings who were somehow entangled with the workings of nature was part of a living tradition of superstition and so a 'fairy kingdom' was not the exclusive belief of children. *A Midsummer Night's Dream* is a sophisticated and adult play, both thought-provoking and highly entertaining.

2.2 ORIGIN AND SOURCES

There is some speculation both as to the precise date when Shakespeare wrote *A Midsummer Night's Dream* and to the sources he drew upon for the material of the play. In addition to the probability of the play's having been written for a specific wedding celebration, there is some weight in the argument that Titania's speech in Act II describing atrocious weather conditions relates to the summers of 1594-6 which are on record as having been particularly inclement. Neither the fact that the play itself is in some ways a celebration of marriage or that the summer weather of the play is unseasonal necessarily relates to the play's origin for both are central to the drama as we have it today. We do know, however, that Francis Meres, a contemporary of Shakespeare, includes *A Midsummer Night's Dream* in a list of plays written before 1598 in his book *Palladis Tamia: Wit's Treasury* and that the first printed text dates from 1600 and was likely to have been approved by the playwright or his company.

Shakespeare tended to rely heavily on other sources for the plots of his plays, though his reworking of the material was invariably masterly. The plot of *A Midsummer Night's Dream* for once appears pretty certainly to be almost entirely of his creation. Of the sources that we know to have been available to him, it is certain that he used Thomas North's translation of Plutarch's *Lives* and Geoffrey Chaucer's *Knight's Tale* for the story of Theseus, and Arthur Golding's translation of Ovid's *Metamorphoses* for the tale of Pyramus and Thisbe. We shall be examining other possible sources as they arise in the text of the play but students who are particularly interested in the debates concerning date of composition and likely sources are referred to the discussion in Antony W. Price's book *A Midsummer Night's Dream*, (Casebook Series, Macmillan, London, 1983) or to the introductions to their editions of the play.

2.3 THE PLOT

Shakespeare sets the whole play in the framework of a marriage celebration and presents us with four groups of characters whose fortunes intertwine during the course of the play. The physical setting is ancient Athens and a nearby wood but, as we shall see, both have a great resemblance to Elizabethan England in many respects. In order that the complex structure of the play can be easily followed we shall first focus on the *dramatis personae* – the players as they first appear.

1. **The Athenian Court**
    Theseus, Duke of Athens   whose wedding is about to
    Hippolyta, Queen of the Amazons take place

Philostrate, Master of the Revels
Egeus, complaining father of Hermia
2. **The Lovers**
Hermia, a small, dark-haired girl in love with Lysander
Lysander, in love with Hermia but disapproved of by Egeus, her father
Demetrius, also in love with Hermia and supported by Egeus
Helena, a tall blonde girl in love with Demetrius
3. **The 'mechanicals'**: a group of artisans who are rehearsing a play to present at Theseus's wedding.
Peter Quince, a carpenter
Nick Bottom, a weaver
Francis Flute, a bellows-mender
Tom Snout, a tinker
Robin Starveling, a tailor
Snug, a joiner
4. **The Immortals**
Oberon, King of the Fairies
Puck (Robin Goodfellow), a knavish spirit loyal to Oberon
Titania, Queen of the Fairies, currently disputing the ownership of a changeling child with Oberon
Pease-blossom
Cobweb   Fairies loyal to Titania
Moth
Mustardseed

Already we can see that each group has within it sources of dramatic tension even before the groups interact: these can be summarised as:

The Court
1. Theseus and Hippolyta are likely to be preoccupied with arrangements for their wedding – traditionally a cause of anxiety and frustration!

The Lovers
2. Two men are in love with the same woman.
3. Helena's love for Demetrius is no longer returned.

The Mechanicals
4. Anyone who has been involved in amateur dramatics will know the tensions of rehearsal that Quince and his friends will experience.

The Fairies
5. Disputed custody of children is now an all-too-familiar aspect of a broken relationship.

To these tensions belonging to particular groups we must add:
6. Egeus does not approve of his daughter's love affair with Lysander;

he would much rather that she married Demetrius.

As the action of the play progresses, other tensions are revealed and these sustain the interest of the audience to the conclusion. It will be helpful now to consider an *outline* of the plot so that the various interweaving strands can be detected. It is a wonderfully inventive plot, full of unexpected twists and it is interesting to note that the main 'plot' really ends with Act IV.

2.4 PLOT SUMMARY

Theseus, Duke of Athens, has defeated Hippolyta, warrior Queen of the Amazons, in battle yet he has now arranged to marry her. He is longing for his wedding and has ordered the beginning of festivities but is asked to arbitrate in the dispute between Egeus and his daughter Hermia. Egeus insists that Hermia should marry Demetrius but Hermia is deeply in love with Lysander. The Athenian law exacts terrible penalties from daughters who disobey their fathers and Theseus gives Hermia a few days to change her mind.

The situation is so intolerable for Hermia and Lysander that they decide to run away together through the woods to the safety of another city-state with different laws and they reveal this plan to one of Hermia's old school friends, Helena. Helena, however, is violently in love with Demetrius who was once in love with her. She therefore betrays her friend's confidence and decides to use this information in a last attempt to gain the attention of Demetrius. Accordingly, when night falls, all four young people are in the woods: Hermia and Lysander fleeing Athens, Demetrius in pursuit of *them* and Helena in pursuit of *him*.

It is to the woods that a group of artisans have gone to rehearse their play, a version of the story of Pyramus and Thisbe. Under the direction of Peter Quince, the carpenter, this inexperienced company is having difficulty in mastering even the basic skills of stagecraft. The exception is Nick Bottom, a self-confident and flamboyant character who fancies himself as an actor and wants to play all the best parts; Quince deals with him firmly and sends the company away to learn their lines by the next rehearsal.

The woods are also the haunt of the fairies and the scene of the fierce dispute between Oberon and Titania over the custody of a changeling child. Already Nature reflects this quarrel with terrible weather and their exchanges grow ever more bitter with wild accusations on both sides.

Oberon hatches a plot with his attendant Puck, a great practical joker. Puck is to obtain a juice from a particular flower which when squeezed onto a sleeper's eyelids will make that person fall hopelessly in love with the next living being he or she sees. The idea is that Titania will be tricked in this way to fall in love with some hideous creature and out of love with the changeling boy.

Fairies can be invisible to mortals and Oberon is able to witness the behaviour of the four lovers who have come to the wood. He first observes Demetrius who is trying both to catch up with Hermia and Lysander and to shake off a very persistent Helena. Demetrius has reached a stage of sheer exasperation with Helena who is throwing herself at him quite openly. Oberon determines to use the 'love juice' to remedy the situation and orders Puck to use the juice on Demetrius once he, himself, has applied it to Titania's eyes.

The complications which follow this decision are hilarious to watch but painful for the characters. Puck first mistakes Lysander and Hermia, who are sleeping on the ground, for Demetrius and Helena. Lysander awakes just as Helena enters the part of the wood where he is sleeping and falls instantly in love with her. Realising his mistake, Puck applies the juice to Demetrius's eyes with the result that both men are madly in love with Helena. Such a change in her fortunes is made all the more painful by the furious onslaught of Hermia who finds herself without a lover and the situation is only resolved when Puck induces sleep in them all and pairs off Hermia with Lysander and Helena with Demetrius.

It can be helpful to represent this part of the plot with diagrams as follows:

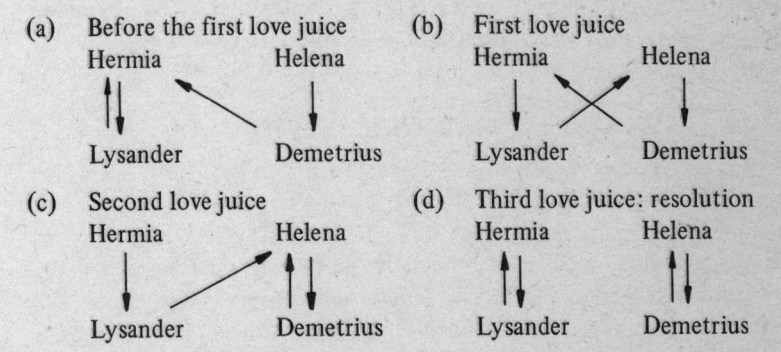

(a) Before the first love juice
Hermia ⇅ Lysander   Helena ↙↓ Demetrius

(b) First love juice
Hermia ↓⤫ Lysander   Helena ↓ Demetrius

(c) Second love juice
Hermia ↓ Lysander   Helena ⇅↗ Demetrius

(d) Third love juice: resolution
Hermia ⇅ Lysander   Helena ⇅ Demetrius

The lovers are woken by the sound of hunting horns as Theseus, Hippolyta and Egeus are taking some early morning sport in the woods. At the sight of the two couples Theseus decides to override Egeus's objections to his daughter's wishes and suggests that both couples are married at the same time as Hippolyta and himself.

The 'Mechanicals' meet for their second rehearsal at a place in the wood near Titania's bower. All goes well until Puck, who has been watching the rehearsal with great amusement, fixes an ass's head on Bottom as he is about to make a dramatic entrance. The cast run off in terror leaving a bemused Bottom to comfort himself by singing; but his musical efforts wake Titania and as she is under the influence of the 'love juice' she finds him irresistible. She orders her fairies to pamper him and eventually she takes him to her bower.

Oberon has his way: his Queen yields to his taunts, he releases her from the spell and they are reconciled. Bottom, too, is released just in time for him to star in a farcical performance of 'Pyramus and Thisbe' at the multiple wedding celebrations. As the three couples retire to bed the Fairies visit the house to bless the marriages and to celebrate the return of harmony.

A note on time-scale and scenes

The opening speech of the play indicates that four days are to pass before the wedding of Theseus and Hippolyta but the action of the play only represents three days. This discrepancy passes unnoticed in performance and may well be the sort of inconsistency that a playwright working under intense pressure would allow. Almost certainly, the play is intended to be played without an interval and the National Theatre Company recently demonstrated how effective that can be.

Since the eighteenth century it has been usual for 'scenes' in printed plays to indicate a change of physical location but prior to that a fresh 'scene' began whenever a new character entered or a character left the stage. It is useful to think of a play as being composed of such units and in the summaries which follow there is an indication of this division.

2.5 SCENE SUMMARIES AND CRITICAL COMMENTARY

Act I, Scene i

Summary

The stage represents Theseus's court; Theseus and Hippolyta are looking forward to their wedding in four days' time when the new moon will appear. Theseus orders celebrations throughout Athens but the mood is changed by the entrance of Egeus 'full of vexation' with his daughter Hermia and two young men, Lysander and Demetrius. Egeus wishes Hermia to marry Demetrius and accuses Lysander of having so 'bewitched' her with lovers' devices that she is determined to disobey her father and marry Lysander. Theseus lectures Hermia on obedience to her father and confirms that Egeus may demand the death penalty but he adds that Hermia might have the alternative of being forced to become a nun.

Demetrius and Lysander each attempt to sway the argument in their favour and Lysander reveals that Demetrius had once loved Helena. Admitting that he had heard as much, Theseus takes Egeus and Demetrius off stage for some 'private schooling'.

Hermia and Lysander are left to ruminate on the pains of love and the difficulty of their situation, then Lysander reveals his plan that they should elope together through the woods to the house of an aunt who lives beyond the reach of the 'sharp Athenian law'. Hermia promises to meet Lysander by night but at this point Helena enters complaining at Demetrius's treatment of her and envying Hermia's ability to appear so attractive to him. Hermia and Lysander try to comfort Helena by revealing to her their plan to leave Athens. Helena is left alone on stage to soliloquise self-pityingly about the problems of love and in her determination to win back Demetrius's favour she decides to tell him of her friends' plan.

By the end of this scene we have been introduced to two of the four sets of characters in the play.

Commentary

The scene falls naturally into five units each with its distinctive changes of pace and mood: the relaxed and joyful anticipation of marriage (1-19); Egeus's complaint and the tension it creates (20-127); the tenderness and renewed hope of two lovers (128-179); attempts to comfort an old friend (180-225) and Helena's soliloquy (226-251). The opening establishes the theme of love and its consummation in marriage; the language is lyrical, courtly and rich in imagery. As Theseus and Hippolyta anticipate their wedding there is a contrast between their impatient desire and the slow passage of time. This is achieved partly by the nature of the language where the long vowel sounds drag down the pace, for example, 'how slow this old moon wanes' (3-4); the choice of words such as 'lingers', and the effective image of a young heir waiting for his inheritance. Even Hippolyta's suggestion that the time will pass quickly reinforces the dream-like and romantic quality of this exchange and from the opening of the play we see the predominant role of the moon both as a marker of time, a bringer of romance and an image of Diana, goddess of chastity and a huntress whose bow is soon to be 'New-bent in heaven' (10).

The rhythm of the action changes sharply with the entry of Egeus and the three lovers: Egeus hardly pauses until he has reeled off the whole of his complaint. The atmosphere of happiness is now threatened by Egeus's description of another facet of love, the secret courtship of young people. In contrast to Theseus's formal wooing of Hippolyta following his conquest of her in battle, Lysander has 'bewitched' Hermia with tokens of young love by moonlight. Note the built-in stage directions as Egeus demands that Demetrius and Lysander 'stand forth' in turn, thus enabling the audience to identify them, and also that Egeus's demand for the death sentence would have struck an Elizabethan audience as less harsh than it does us with our more liberal views of parental authority. Theseus's gentle lecture on this subject provokes terse and uncompromising answers from Hermia but the scene takes on a chilling note when Theseus outlines the punishment for disobedience.

Much of the play is to revolve around the problems of 'judgment' and 'looking' (see 56 and 57) and this is ironically foreshadowed in the two lines preceding Hermia's question as to her fate. In Theseus's answer the moon, which has promised such fulfilment in the opening lines of the play, becomes an image of coldness, barrenness and enforced chastity – a state which is contrasted later with the *elected* chastity of Diana and Elizabeth the virgin queen. A reinforcing image is that of the rose which yields its scent when plucked better than if left to wither and die on the bush; Lysander seems to refer back to this when he asks Hermia

> Why is your cheek so pale?
> How chance the roses there do fade so fast? (128-9)

Theseus is mitigating Egeus's demands so far as he feels he can by setting the time for Hermia's decision by the next new moon, the day of his own marriage, and his appeal for reflection in the face of headstrong impatience derives from his own disciplined approach to love. His pronouncement (83-90) makes the scene explode with energy – it has, in effect, become a trial scene and the disputants each press their case. Lysander is sarcastic and plays his trump card when mentioning Demetrius's former love of Helena. His repetition of 'dotes' (108-9) in his description of Helena's affection emphasises her predicament and emotion as a jilted lover and prepares us for her entrance later in the scene. The effect on Theseus raises some fascinating questions: does he take Egeus and Demetrius off for some 'private schooling' because, having admitted that he *had* heard of Demetrius's affair, he now seeks to change their minds? If so, why then does he so sharply remind Hermia of her duty? The 'Arden' edition defines 'schooling' as 'admonition' which implies more than simple advice.

At the point of his exit Theseus suddenly notices Hippolyta (122) who has remained silent throughout. This provides a problem for the actress playing her as to what her reactions have been. (A similar example of an acting problem occurs in the opening of the scene where the actor playing Theseus must show some reaction to Hippolyta's words *before* he orders Philostrate to organise revels (11).) From Theseus's 'What cheer, my love?' (122) we can see that Hippolyta is disturbed by what she has witnessed. *She* has been promised a wedding day of which the revelry will lift the shadow of former injuries, and now that wedding day will blight another woman's love.

The mood and pace change markedly when Hermia and Lysander are left alone; unlike the public declaration of love by Theseus and Hippolyta the exchange between the two young lovers is private, intimate and passionate. Their defiance gives way to concern for each other as they reflect on the agonies of love. There always seems to be some impediment and the emotion of the scene is heightened by their speaking alternate lines (a technique known as stichomythia) in which they seek to find new ways of expressing their thoughts. It is at the point of climax and resigation that Lysander's plan for escape is revealed and draws from Hermia a gently teasing but elaborate vow of constancy spoken in rhymed couplets. This verbal patterning, familiar to Elizabethans as a rhetorical device, gives an added sense of courtly love to the relationship. Shakespeare also employs stichomythia for the sympathetic discussion between Hermia and Helena and its effect here is to emphasise the frustration of the situation.

The entry of Helena is an example of Shakespeare's stagecraft as she is seen approaching and is introduced to the audience by name (179); Hermia's pun on 'fair', intended at this point as a comment on her beauty, is later seen also to refer to the fact that Helena is blonde and Hermia dark. Helena's first lines concentrate entirely on the nature of *physical attraction* – a quality she longs to learn from Hermia and the entire conversation with Hermia highlights the strength, pain and paradox of unrequited love. A deeply romantic atmosphere is extended by the beautiful image of Phoebe the moon, with which Lysander describes the escape plan, but Helena is unable to speak until Lysander and Hermia have gone, such is her misery in the face of their happiness, which reveals itself in their excited, breathless exit.

Helena' soliloquy extends the theme of physical attraction for she reflects that this apparently straightforward phenomenon is distorted by love: what the person in love sees and what everyone else sees are quite different; love so changes human perception that it *transforms* so that it is really the *imagination* which sees and not the eye. *These are key concepts for the remainder of the play* and we shall return to Helena's speech (226–51) for clues as to the meaning of the subsequent action. Throughout the scene we have seen characters aware of constraints: the constraint of decorum as Theseus and Hippolyta await the freedom to consummate their love in marriage; the constraint of a father's will and the law from which Lysander and Hermia will seek freedom in the woods. These constraints also set up the tensions in the plot, especially as Helena finds the constraint of friendship overruled by her desire for Demetrius. This is the last time for a long while that we see the lovers in the rational daylight of Theseus' court; the moonlit wood to which they move becomes a place of transformation and disorder.

Act I, Scene ii

Summary

A group of Athenian workmen led by Peter Quince meet at an unspecified location in the town to prepare a play for performance at Theseus's wedding. The parts for the play – a version of the story of Pyramus and Thisbe – are distributed among these amateur actors of whom Bottom shows himself to be the most self-confident and dominant. Bottom, in fact, wants to play all the roles but Quince convinces him that he must stick to Pyramus.

The workmen (the third group of characters) agree to have their next rehearsal in the woods outside the town.

Commentary

This is the first scene of pure comedy in the play and the prose in which it is written contrasts with the more elaborate and sophisticated verse of the previous scene. The comedy derives not only from the comic characters, each of whom has a name appropriate to his trade, but also from the fact that they take themselves very seriously. Shakespeare also creates a great deal of humour by his parody of amateur acting and of some of the theatre practices of his day. This is examined in some detail in section 4.6, '*A Midsummer Night's Dream* in the Theatre' but it is important to note here that performances of the play can be ruined by too obvious 'clowing' on the part of the Mechanicals.

The play being rehearsed by Quince and his friends is *The Most Lamentable Comedy and Most Cruel Death of Pyramus and Thisbe*. It is sometimes referred to as an 'interlude' (6), which in Tudor times was a common name for a short play, often to be performed in a great house. Its extraordinary title suggests a strange blend of comedy and tragedy and is particularly appropriate because *A Midsummer Night's Dream* itself, whilst remaining a comedy could, if Egeus's wishes had prevailed, have had a tragic element. The Mechanicals' interlude is, in fact, about young lovers thwarted by their parents' interference and therefore will present a version of what *might* have happened to Hermia and Lysander.

Although these simple artisans speak prose both Quince (7) and Bottom (53, 81 and 102) make laughable errors in their attempts to express themselves in florid sentences. In spite of his malapropisms (using words incorrectly) Bottom dominates the scene, giving a demonstration of his emotional range as a ranting actor by bursting into bombastic verse – he has all the swagger of an amateur 'ham' with some knowledge of plays and the theatre. The other characters are each given sufficient interesting characteristics to make a comic blend; Flute, with his piping voice and only just growing facial hair, is as shy as Bottom is confident; Quince is intelligent enough to get what he wants from Bottom (notice his clever flattery in 84-7) and quick-witted enough to make a bawdy joke out of Bottom's list of beards (95-6); Snug knows himself to be slow-witted. The roles assigned to Snout and Starveling do not materialise in the eventual performance – another of Shakespeare's inconsistencies which passes virtually unnoticed.

This group of characters also feels the constraints of the town and decides to seek the freedom of the woods, setting its time also by moonlight.

Act II, Scene i

Summary

In this scene we are introduced to the fourth group of characters: the Fairies and their world. The opening lines are an exchange between a fairy, who serves Titania, and Puck, or Robin Goodfellow, the 'shrewd and knavish sprite' who is loyal to Oberon. We learn of the quarrel that has developed between the Fairy King and Queen concerning the custody of an Indian boy and of the tricks which Puck likes to play on mortals.

Oberon and Titania enter from opposite sides of the stage and their meeting is stormy: they accuse each other of having emotional entanglements with Hippolyta and Theseus and in a long speech Titania explains that the whole natural world has been upset by their quarrel. Oberon replies that the remedy is hers – she need only hand over the Indian boy. She refuses and leaves the stage.

Oberon now reveals part of his plan to Puck; he sends Puck to fetch a flower of which the juice has the effect of making people 'dote' on the next person or creature seen, however unattractive they may be. He tells the audience how he will squeeze the juice into Titania's eye when she is asleep and then force her to give up the boy once she has begun to dote on some absurd being.

At this point Demetrius enters, followed by Helena; Oberon, being invisible, observes them. Demetrius is furious that Helena has pursued him and tries to drive her away with threats of violence but Helena twists all his words and still follows him as he runs from the stage. Oberon, moved by Helena's plight decides to reverse the situation and when Puck returns with the magic juice he describes how he will use some of it on Titania but then sends Puck to find Demetrius in order to squeeze some into his eyes. Oberon does not realise that there is any other young man in the woods so he simply tells Puck to look for 'a disdainful youth' wearing Athenian garments and use the love juice to make him dote on the lady (Helena) and that Puck is to meet Oberon again before dawn.

Commentary

The opening exchange between two 'spirits' serves various purposes: it provides a number of important points in the exposition of the plot and establishes the idea of a Fairy court. The dialogue also serves to heighten the tension which builds towards the entrance of Oberon and Titania.

Our introduction to the Fairies is firstly through Puck, associated in English folklore with Midsummer magic and believed to have dealings with mortals. The Fairy Puck encounters speaks a new verse form with a light rhythm which creates a sense of fluttering movement. Like Puck later in the scene (175), she emphasises the speed with which the Fairies move (7) and the ease with which they travel, for, unlike mortals, they are not earth-bound. These opening lines also change the sense of scale by references to small delicate things such as cowslips and dewdrops and Puck reinforces this as he refers to elves who 'Creep into acorn cups and hide them there' (31). Shakespeare uses rich language to transform a bare stage into a moon-lit wood in our imaginations and it is interesting to note the use he makes of the doors at the rear of the stage.

The essential details of the root of the quarrel between Oberon and Titania are provided by Puck (18-31); Oberon is already described as 'jealous' (24), a label which is used by Titania herself when they meet (61), but it is the anger which the King and Queen of Fairies display at every meeting that disturbs the spirit world. This source of conflict is later seen to disturb the entire natural world and impinge on the lives of mortals, providing also a major springboard for the development of the plot of the play. The effects of Oberon and Titania's quarrel are revealed in their confrontation: the catastrophic nature of these effects derives from their status as King and Queen of Fairies.

We are frequently reminded that there is a 'Fairy court': the cowslips are likened to pensioners (10), (the pensioners were the splendidly attired personal bodyguard of Elizabeth I). Puck suggests that he is a court jester (44), and Oberon later evokes Elizabethan court entertainments (148-52). These and other references are usually taken as a direct compliment to Queen Elizabeth I and the parallel between the Fairy court and the Athenian court has also sometimes led directors to cast the same actor and actress as Oberon and Theseus, Titania and Hippolyta. An argument for this casting would be that the Fairies exist only in the imagination and not in mortal reality.

Before the two major antagonists meet face to face Puck provides an insight into his own character and the Fairy warns us of what is to come

> Are you not he...
> [That] Mislead night-wanderers, laughing at their harm? (39)

The irony of this lingers throughout the play. Puck's involvement with mortals, however, is not vindictive but more like knockabout humour. Its consequences are less far-reaching than Oberon's or Titania's entanglements with humans.

It would be difficult to conceive of more powerful opening lines than those with which Oberon and Titania confront each other from opposite sides of the stage, and their meeting fills the moonlight with tension. As they lash out with their tongues, however, the supernatural powers of the Fairies give way to a lovers' quarrel such as humans have and this is typified by various accusations of unfaithfulness. The fairy and human worlds are brought close together by the suggestions that Oberon and Titania have somehow been involved with Hippolyta and Theseus and this theme is extended in Titania's long and wonderful speech which follows the 'forgeries of jealousy'. The speech (81-117) depicts a natural world upset by their quarrel; a very English picture of wretched summer weather with disastrous consequences for agriculture and sport. A sense of reversal and disorder is created in every line: seasons, whose regularity and recognisable characteristics represent *order* in nature, are confused and 'change their wonted liveries' (112-13), the moon whose power includes the control of tides and floods 'Pale in her anger, washes all the air' (104), and mankind is afflicted with disease.

It is from this speech that some scholars have deduced that Shakespeare is making direct reference to the terrible summer of 1594 but it is important to notice the essential *dramatic* function of the lines at this point in the play. It demonstrates the catastrophic nature of Oberon's and Titania's quarrel, their closeness to the forces of universe and the depth of their feelings. The theme of discord is reinforced and we see that Titania, at least, is very conscious of, and concerned about, the ways in which human life has been affected. In a very striking image Titania makes clear to Oberon the extent of their responsibility for the misfortune that has permeated nature; she refers to a 'progeny of evils' (115) – a child of which they are the parents (117).

The tension of the encounter is maintained by Oberon's sharp reply (118-21) and as always in such quarrels he makes his request *sound* reasonable. To any outside audience, however, neither Titania nor Oberon appears to be behaving in a reasonable manner: the disputed ownership of this particular child should never have provoked such dissension and although Titania's reasons for wanting the child grow from her loyalty to its deceased mother her loyalty to Oberon is strained in the process. The impasse or deadlock which both characters have reached at this point of the play is highlighted by Oberon's refusal to dance (140), Titania's realisation that they are about to quarrel even more violently (145), the memorable couplet with which she sweeps from the stage (144-45), and the taunts Oberon hurls after her (146-7). There is a reminder too in this confrontation that the entire play is set in the context of Theseus's and Hippolyta's wedding (138-9) and this gives an ironic twist to the breakdown of the marriage between their Fairy counterparts.

Oberon's description of the origin of the love juice which will induce 'love at first sight' is a complex mixture of rural and courtly reference. His vision (149-54) in some respects resembles the water-pageants and firework displays with which Queen Elizabeth was entertained when a guest of a great noble, such as those at Kenilworth (1591) and Elvetham (1595). The speech also contains a compliment to Elizabeth 'the imperial vot'ress' (163) who had survived many suitors to acquire a goddess-like status as the 'virgin queen'. This freely chosen virginity contrasts with the enforced virginity which threatens Hermia, and Oberon's speech enhances the honour paid by the play to love consummated in marriage because it is spoken in the awareness of the alternative ideal.

The story of Cupid and the 'little western flower' (166) dignifies the magic agent with an origin of the kind of change or 'metamorphosis' such as might be found in Ovid and from this point 'change' and the sudden impact of Cupid's arrow become major problems in the play. Oberon is established on a higher level of perception than Puck – he says 'I saw – but thou couldst not, (155) but the entire speech creates an atmosphere of mystic magic and we are reminded of the wonderful powers of the Fairies by Puck's promise to

> put a girdle round about the earth
> In forty minutes! (175-6)

Shakespeare gives Oberon a soliloquy (177-85) in which to explain his intentions to the audience: his plan may seem like a cruel trick but it has been made clear that for Titania's good as well as for the order of nature, her obsession must be broken. This means of breaking it is to change it into one so unnatural and absurd that she recognises her own folly. When Oberon's thoughts are interrupted by the entry of Demetrius and Helena he establishes the convention that he is invisible – in the Elizabethan theatre he may well have wrapped a cloak around him when speaking line 186.

The exchange between the two young lovers (188-244) contrasts in language, pace and action with what has gone before. These desperate mortals fling mundane images at each other and chase each other around the stage. Not only does Helena physically follow Demetrius, she turns his insults and threats into expressions of love. This does not come easily to her for her view of women is that they 'were not made to woo' (242) and she feels that the experience she has to go through 'set a scandal on her sex' (240). The extravagances of Helena's attempts to pursue Demetrius outrage her femininity and provoke the sympathy of Oberon but the fast-moving action is very amusing in performance. Some directors, notably Peter Brook, have made Helena *literally* fling herself at Demetrius, reducing her to a man-eating female, but her shyness and discomfort make this a doubtful interpretation. The violence of Demetrius's rejection does, however, make their eventual reconciliation and Helena's faithfulness all the more remarkable and Oberon watching, though still embroiled in his own quarrel, obviously recognises the need to intervene to restore harmony.

Puck's forty-minute journey round the earth is achieved in 'theatre time', that willing suspension of disbelief on the part of the audience that allows the playwright to depart from literalism and telescope events. In another superb moment of his craft Shakespeare has Oberon create one of the most enduring images of the play. His language describing Titania's bower (250-9) is heavy with the scent of flowers, it stresses the bounty of nature with its ideas of sweetness and lusciousness and gives a gentle sense of movement with adjectives such as 'nodding'. Feelings of security are evoked by thoughts of Titania 'overcanopied' and 'lulled' — all these effects add to the purely *visual* impact of Titania's bower (which may well have been seen on the Elizabethan stage because we know that a mossy bank and an arbour were among the large 'props' available in the theatre) and reinforces again the scale and magic of the Fairies' world. Oberon is determined to make Titania 'full of hateful fantasies' (259) — reference to the workings of the imagination which play an increasing part in the subsequent action.

Act II, Scene ii

Summary

For this entire scene the stage represents a part of the moonlit wood which contains a bank graphically described by Oberon in the previous scene. Titania appears with her train of Fairies; they dance and Titania is sung to sleep with a lullaby. Oberon enters, evading the Fairy 'sentinel', and squeezes the love juice in Titania's eyes with an incantation-like verse full of malice. As he leaves, Lysander and Hermia enter, exhausted and lost and they lie down to sleep, Hermia insisting that Lysander keeps proper decorum and lies some distance apart.

Puck enters and what he sees *appears* to confirm what Oberon has said about Demetrius and Helena so he squeezes the juice into Lysander's eyes.

From this point the scene takes on the quality of a farce with characters rushing on and off stage. We briefly glimpse Demetrius as he runs away from Helena, not noticing the very people he is seeking, asleep on the ground. Helena enters, pausing for breath, and wakes Lysander who, being under the influence of the love juice, falls in love with her at once. Helena thinks she is being mocked and tries to leave him but Lysander, stating openly that he now loathes his former beloved Hermia, goes off in pursuit. This leaves Hermia to wake from a nightmare, bewildered. Finding Lysander gone she is terrified and goes off in search of him.

Commentary

Shakespeare captures the interest of the audience by a variety of styles of entertainment in this scene. There are several fascinating changes of pace: at first the relaxed rhythm of the Fairy dance and song, the dreaminess of the lullaby followed by the moment of tension as Oberon squeezes the love juice into Titania's eye. Then the entry of Hermia and Lysander, weary and slow because they are exhausted and lost (41-4) contrasting sharply with that of Demetrius and Helena (89) invariably running and breathless (44) or with the sudden awakening of Hermia later in the scene (151). The text itself contains clues for the action: Titania must remain asleep on stage until III. i, possibly in the 'discovery space' at the rear of the stage; Lysander must eventually sleep well away from Hermia so that Puck thinks he has come across Demetrius still refusing to have anything to do with Helena (see 50, 70 and 75-80); Hermia awakes violently, imagining a serpent at her throat (44) and some directors have taken Oberon's evasion of the 'sentinel' to mean that some of his followers 'kidnap' the Fairy - the line 'One aloof stand sentinel' (32) certainly suggests that the Fairy would have been positioned on some upper level or balcony.

The nature of the Fairies, particularly their tiny scale, is established by Titania's set of instructions for tasks of minute delicacy (1-7) to be accomplished in 'the third part of a minute'. The caring and protective attitude to the Queen is symbolised in the dance and song which provide another mode of enjoyment for the audience and Oberon only evades the charm because what he does will eventually work for Titania's good, not her harm.

Much of the scene derives its impact from its accurate and sometimes comic portrayal of the behaviour of young lovers. Hermia and Lysander are at odds because Lysander wishes to sleep close beside his love. She, in turn, considers this too 'forward' and the puns and protests turn this familiar situation into comedy. Demetrius is too desperate to notice the very people he is seeking asleep on the stage and Helena is too distraught to see them either - she is more concerned to blame Hermia's flashing eyes for her troubles (compare I, i, 184) and to conclude that she, herself, is ugly. This typical behaviour of the jilted lover makes her disbelief at the protestations of Lysander's love more credible. Lysander, 'doting' on Helena, states openly that he now loathes his former beloved Hermia and his wildly exaggerated declarations of love for Helena are a parody of courtly 'romance'.

The irony is that each of the lovers imagines him or herself to be behaving with rationality and reason. Lysander claims that his dotage for Helena is a result of his now having seen *reason* - the frequency with which he repeats the word (120-6) only emphasises the absurdity of his claim for in this scene the lovers are all governed by their emotions. Audience sympathy is undoubtedly with the two women. We can genuinely admire the way in which Helena handles the situation following Lysander's declaration of love and Hermia awakes from one nightmare to find herself in another; the audience are aware of the painful discovery about the unfaithfulness of her lover which she has yet to make. It is as if dreams are already proving more reliable guides to the truth than 'reality' and reason.

Amongst all the changing fortunes of the scene it is worth noting Shakespeare's superb artistry in creating theatrical atmosphere in a single statement: 'Night and silence' (76).

Act III, Scene i

Summary

Quince, with his group of amateur actors, has chosen the same spot in the wood for his rehearsal and there is no break in the action between this and the previous scene. Titania still sleeps at the rear of the stage as the Mechanicals enter, remarking on the suitability of the place with a natural acting area and a hawthorn bush from behind which they can make their entrances. Progress is slow because of the actors' inexperience: they worry that the deaths and roaring lion in their play will terrify the ladies in the audience and are equally troubled as to how to bring a real wall and moonlight onto the stage. When they have found solutions to these problems Puck enters in time to see Quince starting to direct the rehearsal. Various absurd mistakes are made and Puck finds these very amusing. Just as Bottom is about to make an entrance as Pyramus from behind the hawthorn bush Puck puts an ass's head on him and the cast scatter in terror.

Bottom thinks this an elaborate practical joke so walks up and down singing; his singing, however, wakes Titania who immediately falls in love with him. She uses her magic power to prevent his leaving the wood and calls Fairies to wait on him and bring him gifts. Bottom remains remarkably composed and 'holds court' with the Fairies before Titania has him led to her bower.

Commentary

All the characters in this scene are involved in aspects of change. Bottom and Flute mispronounce words so as to entirely change their meaning. The amateur actors struggle with the problem of dramatic illusion only to be confronted with a more disturbing experience in the transformation of Bottom. Puck, who is responsible for this metamorphosis wonderfully captured in the lines

O Bottom, thou art changed.   (112)

and

> Bless thee, Bottom, bless thee! Thou are translated. (116)

is already known to be an expert at changing his own form in order to play practical jokes on mortals (see II.i.45-57). He considers Bottom to be the most stupid of all the company (see III.ii.13) and thus his changing him quite literally into an ass is appropriate. This may be amusing to Puck, who derives his greatest sport from the misfortunes of mortals, but the Fairies do not escape the power of change. Titania, now under a charm, transfers her affection to Bottom and her infatuation through the senses of sight and sound brings to mind Helena's comment

> Things base and vile, holding no quantity,
> Love can transpose to form and dignity. (I.i.232-3)

In the light of his changed circumstances Bottom responds with a remarkable composure and his down-to-earth comments and the practical use he suggests for Cobweb – to bind up a cut – and Mustardseed – to eat with roast beef – are typical of his prosaic approach which makes Titania's poetic fantasy ridiculous.

This contrast between prose and poetry permeates the scene. The Mechanicals speak prose except when they speak the lines of their play, presumably written by Quince, which have the *form* of verse but none of the *quality* of poetry. They lack poetic imagination and therefore fail to understand that in the theatre an illusion is created in which reality is *represented*. The way in which the Mechanicals eventually reach some measure of understanding in this direction is extremely amusing and it is ironic that Bottom, who has made some perceptive points about actors not actually being what they seem, suddenly appears utterly changed, his entrance timed to follow a reference to a horse! Shakespeare obviously felt that one experience of the lines spoken by the Mechanicals was enough for his audience and in the actual performance in Act V the passage rehearsed in the woods is not repeated.

The collision between the refined imagination and the grossness of prosaic mortality is highlighted in the moments when Bottom enters the delicacy of the Fairy world. Not only is there a marked contrast in language and scale but also in taste and sophistication. The inappropriate absurdity of Titania's words when she is woken by the raucous, tuneless singing of Bottom provides one of the funniest moments in the play (36) and the Queen obviously finds him increasingly noisy as she commands him to be brought 'silently' in the final line of the scene.

In this encounter, however, Bottom shows that Puck was wrong to consider him stupid for he makes the perceptive remark that 'reason and love keep little company together nowadays' (143). This shows a far greater grasp of reality than the deluded Lysander was capable of demonstrating in the previous scene for all his sophistication and appeal to reason. Titania, likewise, provides an impressive and beautiful picture of her special relationship with nature

> I am a spirit of no common rate,
> The summer still doth tend upon my state,   (153-4)

but she is subject to the power of love and its delusions. The romantic images with which Titania surrounds Bottom are themselves of doubtful permanence and though she takes her lover to her bower under the eye of the water moon the *comic* image of an amateur actor representing the moon is, in the end, more lasting. Bottom, the only mortal in the play to see the Fairy kingdom, knows that it is the wood which is affecting him and hopes he has the wit to get out of it, but his ability as an actor enables him to cope with his change of role. The moonlit farce which he has been rehearsing with his friends is no more absurd than the moonlight drama of Lysander or Titania.

Act III, Scene ii

Summary
When Oberon enters at the opening of the scene *the audience* already knows the result of the love juice on Titania but he is still wondering about it. He hasn't long to wait, however, for Puck bursts in and tells him in a vivid speech of the chaos he has caused amongst the Mechanicals and of how Titania is in love 'with a monster'. Oberon is delighted and is assured by Puck that he has also put the love juice onto Demetrius's eyes.

At this moment Demetrius and Hermia enter – Oberon recognises Demetrius but not Hermia, but he has no time to speak so he and Puck observe unseen. Demetrius is making declarations of love but Hermia responds bitterly and accuses Demetrius of having murdered Lysander. Finally losing her temper, Hermia storms from the stage and Demetrius, overcome with exhaustion, sinks down to sleep.

Oberon realises Puck's mistake and speaks sharply to him. Puck goes to find Helena who, Oberon tells him, is pale and sighing, whilst the King of Fairies squeezes love juice into Demetrius's eyes with some magic words. Puck achieves his mission in a few seconds and announces the approach of Helena and Lysander.

As they enter Helena is still followed by Lysander swearing himself to be in love with her. Helena tries to rebuff him but their argument wakes Demetrius who, seeing Helena, makes extravagant declarations of love towards her. This is too much for Helena who thinks it all part of an elaborate trick to mock her: she appeals to their manliness, accuses them of misusing a woman and is unable to keep back her tears. The men turn on each other in jealous rivalry and, attracted by the sound of Lysander's voice, Hermia enters. She is relieved to see Lysander and asks why he had left her but he replies that he has transferred his affection to Helena. Helena sees this as only another part of the trick being played on her and, suspecting Hermia of complicity, reminds her of their lifelong friendship. Hermia is bewildered but his only enrages Helena, who makes as if to leave. A quarrel now breaks out between the two men and Hermia tries to restrain Lysander. He pushes her away with insults and she realises that she has, indeed, lost his love. This causes her to turn on Helena who promptly joins in the taunts about Hermia's small stature. Furiously Hermia displays her temper and seems likely to attack Helena. Lysander is now free from Hermia's grasp and challenges Demetrius to settle their differences in a dual. The two men leave the stage; Helena, afraid to be left alone with Hermia also exits, followed by Hermia.

Oberon, having watched all this, accuses Puck of negligence but Puck claims that it was a genuine mistake. Oberon gives orders that Puck should cause such thick fog that the two men will lost each other — he is to lead them on by imitating their voices till they fall asleep with exhaustion and Puck can then put love-juice in Lysander's eyes in order to restore harmony. Morning is approaching fast and Puck realises that his task must be accomplished quickly. Oberon leaves the stage and each of the lovers in turn reappears until all four are sleeping on stage. Puck now squeezes the juice in Lysander's eye and the audience knows that when the lovers wake they will have only a dreamlike recollection of the night's events.

Commentary

During this scene, the longest in the play, the plots of the lovers, the Mechanicals and the Fairies all pass through a state of confusion, though it is only through reported action that the audience is reminded of Bottom and Titania. Puck likens the confused Mechanicals to wild geese and jackdaws noisily wheeling about the sky scared by the report of a gun and this image could well apply to the behaviour of the lovers, especially at the close of the scene when Puck leads Lysander and Demetrius through the dark. Quince and his friends were so panic-striken when they saw Bottom transformed that they have imagined harmless things to be terrible and have fled into the bushes, tumbling over and trying to disentangle themselves from the briars. Similarly, the lovers find themselves in an extension of the 'night-rule' (6) of Puck in which mistakes, illusions and passions fall over each other.

When Demetrius and Hermia first enter they have obviously been talking for some time and Demetrius has been making passionate declarations of love. Hermia, however, can only account for the disappearance of Lysander by thinking that she sees in Demetrius's intense looks the expression of a murderer. Her confusion is appreciated by the audience when she states

> The sun was not so true unto the day
> As he to me. Would he have stol'n away
> From sleeping Hermia?   (50–3)

but such unexpected reversals are the result of irrational love. Demetrius's confusion is as real because he does not know what has happened to Lysander. As the anxiety and desperation of the characters increase, so their emotions show themselves. Hermia explodes with anger, revealing a fearsome temper when Demetrius lets slip his first vicious indication of jealous hatred for Lysander (64).

The climax of the scene is reached when all four lovers are brought on stage together with the second entry of Hermia (176) and it is important to grasp the basis of the dramatic tension and comic action for the ensuing confrontation. All the characters have their own problems and aims: **Hermia** has been searching for Lysander and her first reaction is that, at last, she has found him. Her first ten speeches reveal utter confusion at her reception and the behaviour of the other three. At one point she also thinks Lysander is joking. Her aim remains the recapture of Lysander and it is only after genuine questioning that she turns in fury on Helena (286), accusing her of stealing her love. Together with the terrible change that has come over Lysander she is also baffled by the fact that when she last met Demetrius, he was making love to *her*.

Helena is convinced from Hermia's first words that she, too, has joined in the planning of this unkind joke – though secretly she may feel that she has brought the situation on herself by revealing Hermia's and Lysander's plan in the first place. It is all the more painful for both women because, as close school friends, they shared their secrets and now Helena feels utterly alone, with no idea what she can do.

Lysander must be embarrassed by the presence of Hermia and, as so often happens in such situations, treats her abominably. He is also sickened by Demetrius who has continued to be his rival by once again changing the object of his affections. Lysander's behaviour is aggressive but interspersed with attempts to remind Demetrius that *he* can now have Hermia and to convince Helena that he loves her. He cannot understand Demetrius's change of heart.

Demetrius realises now that his infatuation with Hermia was a foolish, temporary thing and that he has really loved Helena all along. Indeed, he loves her constantly from now on. His situation is greatly complicated by the unreasonable behaviour of Lysander who, not content with taking Hermia to the brink of marriage, has now started an affair with Helena. His aim must be to regain Helena's esteem and ward off Lysander.

The interaction of these four characters with their conflicting aims is made very amusing for the audience who know the true cause of their behaviour. The scene is often played very boisterously with much of the humour coming from the almost pantomime-like action. It can be a very physical scene with Hermia desperately clinging on to Lysander (he calls her a 'burr' in 262) and then trying to attack the timid Helena while the two men try to fend her off. Meanwhile, the two men try to gain the attention of Helena by, perhaps, kneeling at her feet and kissing her hands whilst threatening each other with violence. As the scene grows more passionate the contact between the two women, the short, dark, fiery Hermia and the tall, fair, timid Helena becomes another source of humour for the audience but an excuse for vicious insults between the characters.

In all the exchanges between the lovers in III.ii we sense a lack of control. This is first revealed in the elaborate verbal conceits (clever witticisms) and images with which the men, particularly, express themselves. Courtiers of Elizabeth's time would have been familiar with the rhetorical devices which form the basis of the lover's dialogue but the extravagant declarations of love have a false ring. Lysander protests that his vows are accompanied by real tears (123) and says that he had no 'judgment' when he made love to Hermia, whereas Demetrius praises Helena's eyes, lips and hands for their exquisite beauty only a short time after rebuffing her (137-44). Matters grow worse when the two women clash directly and Helena, who earlier has given an idealised view of their school days (202-16), descends into cattiness by dredging up Hermia's youthful reputation as a 'vixen'. Their quarrel sinks to the level of cutting personal remarks about appearance and all four lovers leave the stage in a state of anger, dismay and confusion.

In complete contrast, the audience senses throughout the potential control of Oberon. When he realises Puck's mistake, his strong reprimand of short, monosyllabic words 'What hast thou done?' (87) stamps his authority and changes the pace of the scene after Demetrius's sleepy rhythm. Swift, urgent and purposeful, Puck is sent on his way but he comments on the waywardness of mankind: fate has decreed that for every man who holds good to his vows (troth - the word still used in the promises at many marriage services) there are a million who break them, even though they have sworn time after time (92-3). Both Demetrius (before the play began) and now Lysander are among the million.

Oberon's control is prompted by his concern for mortals: his intervention was initiated by his sympathy for Helena and it is certainly not his intention that Lysander or Demetrius should come to harm. The remedy for the present problem brings from Oberon a wonderfully atmospheric evocation of darkness in which the long vowel sounds slow the entire stage action and the audience senses the change of light and the approach of 'death counterfeiting sleep':

> Hie therefore, Robin, overcast the night.
> The starry welkin cover thou anon
> With drooping fog as black as Acheron,   (362-4)

Such control over the world of nature is possible only because Oberon and Puck are remarkable spirits. They remind the audience that daylight, is approaching and with it reason. 'Aurora's harbinger', the morning star is already in the sky and the ghostly, evil spirits who haunt the night are returning to their graves. 'But *we*', says Oberon, 'are spirits of *another* sort' (395); positive powers of good. Oberon's subsequent speech (396-400) is not simply a most beautiful word-painting of a sunrise that more than compensates for the absence of stage lighting, it is also a remarkable demonstration of the Fairies' unique relationship with the wonders of nature. His claim: 'I with the morning's love have oft made sport' (396) can be interpreted literally in either of two ways: he has actually made love to the goddess Aurora *or* he has hunted with Aurora's lover Cephalus but beyond this Oberon is saying that, in some mystical way, he and nature are part of the same scheme of things.

The 'fond pageant' which has provided Puck and the audience with so much amusement is finally manipulated by Oberon to resolve the lovers' problems. The characters have had enough of darkness and their words express this as they enter and sleep. As Puck prepares for the pathetic entrance of Hermia he shows some sympathy, as the audience must, with those who are afflicted by a force they cannot control. It was Cupid's arrow which fell on the flower to produce the love juice and yet, ironically, it was by Cupid's bow that Hermia swore to Lysander (I.i.169). Mortals, however, never know when they will be struck by love for, as Helena has reminded us (I.i.235), Cupid aims blind. Hermia who, like Helena, has remained faithful to the end shows true love's durability by tenderly thinking of Lysander before she sleeps, in spite of the dreadful treatment he has handed out to her.

The restoration of harmony for the lovers is finalised by Puck in a simple rhyme of great delicacy and gentleness (457-72) ending appropriately in a proverb from folklore, which traditionally links the human and spirit worlds. So the elaborate and contorted expressions, the bitterness, the confusion, the desperate running and shouting are replaced by tranquillity.

Act IV, Scene i

Summary
The four lovers remain asleep on stage for the first part of this scene and

we also discover later that during the time which has elapsed since we last saw Bottom and Titania, Oberon has met them and taunted Titania so cruelly about her new love that she has given him the changeling child, almost as a peace offering. We also hear that when Oberon found Titania with Bottom she had crowned him with flowers so it is reasonable to suppose that when Bottom enters with Titania and some Fairies at the opening of this scene he is still wearing a garland.

Titania strokes Bottom's cheeks and kisses his ears while he asks Peaseblossom to scratch his head, Cobweb to bring honey from a bee and Mustardseed to join in the scratching. Titania offers him music and food but after showing a preference for crude versions of both Bottom feels sleepy and rests in the entwining arms of Titania.

Oberon, who has been watching, comes forward and tells Puck what has taken place between Titania and himself, then he squeezes the antidote into Titania's eye. Titania wakes and is horrified to recall her love for Bottom. Oberon tells Puck to remove Bottom's ass head while he himself dances with Titania to magic music. Morning is fast approaching and the Fairies leave the stage; the sound of hunting horns is heard and Theseus enters with Hippolyta, Egeus and members of the court. On this their wedding day Thesus and Hippolyta discuss hounds and hunting but Theseus notices the sleeping lovers. He gives orders for them to be woken with the blowing of horns and comments on the new-found harmony which appears to exist between the lovers. The lovers try to explain what has happened and Demetrius admits that he no longer loves Hermia. Theseus postpones further discussion and decrees that he will override Egeus's wishes and that the two couples are to be married in a triple ceremony with Hippolyta and himself. He leaves the stage with his court, and the four lovers, still wondering if they are asleep or dreaming, follow.

This leaves Bottom, who has not been noticed and as he wakes he imagines he is still rehearsing. Finding himself alone he also recalls the night's events like a dream and goes off to ask Quince to write a ballad about it.

Commentary
For Titania, Bottom and the lovers this scene marks a return from fantasy to reality, an awaking from a dream. Titania's dream, like Hermia's earlier in the play, has a nightmarish quality: her passion for Bottom reaches the height of absurdity as she praises his most ridiculous physical features and caresses him as if he were the most desirable of men. The incongruity of the clumsiest of mortals transformed into the most inelegant of beasts, surrounded by delicate Fairies is highlighted by the gracious but entirely inappropriate replies Bottom makes to every remark of Titania and the

final moments of her dream consist of murmuring words of passionate love into Bottom's enormous ears!

The lovers also have been through many troublesome situations and their return to consciousness is confused, Lysander's 'Pardon, my lord' (139) covering a great deal of stage 'business' (actions by the actors). His later attempt to explain the circumstances to Thesus only amplifies the vague frontiers between sleeping, waking, dreaming and reality. Yet Bottom, who has expressed similar confusion on waking, recalls his dream as a 'most rare vision' (201) and the wonder of his experience is such that he wants to preserve it.

The waking of Titania and the lovers is a movement from discord to harmony. Oberon and Titania finding themselves 'new in amity' (86) celebrate with music and dance. These symbols of harmony which Oberon has earlier refused (see II.i.14) occur again when the Fairies give their final blessing to the married couples. The way in which confusion and discord can resolve to produce satisfying music is hinted at by both Hippolyta and Theseus as they discuss their hounds. (When clashing musical notes change to create a beautiful chord we say they 'resolve'.) The music with which the Fairies have induced a deep sleep in the lovers is replaced by a soundscape of the clamour of baying hounds; Theseus refers to this 'musical confusion' (108) and Hippolyta to 'so musical a discord' and 'such sweet thunder' (116). We can detect here a vagueness in the distinctions between discord and harmony similar to that between sleeping and waking.

This scene emphasises that there is no clear cut frontier between the apparent contrasts in the play. At first glance it seems that the entry of Theseus from the daylight world of Athens into Oberon's confused, wooded, night-time domain heralds the return of reason and reality. His first words, consisting of blunt, forthright language, contrast with the elegant rhyming couplets of the Fairies as if poeticism is replaced by common sense and on the surface his logic prevails. But Theseus was unable to suggest an answer to Hermia's problem and it is only when Oberon's control of the imagination has done its work that Theseus finds a ready-made solution in the lovers' 'concord' (141). Similarly, Egeus, who is furious and repeats himself over and over again, has absolute reason on his side, yet having watched the events of the play who would consider his behaviour in this scene 'reasonable'? Theseus embodies this contradiction in his description of his hunting dogs which appear to have been bred far more for their vocal abilities than for their speed. This is a surprising admission on the part of the normally pragmatic Theseus but, as he shows later, he has a sharp appreciation of aesthetic qualities in spite of his logical mind.

The return of reality to the lovers is marked by a complete change of tone in their language. In place of hyperbole (the device of exaggeration for effect), there is a direct sincerity with a total absence of ornament. Demetrius, the only lover to remain permanently affected by the love juice, is the first to speak at length in this way. He realises that he truly loves Helena, not just as an infatuation through the *eye* but as a deep emotion of the heart. He presents his dotage on Hermia as a 'sickness' and the restoration of his love for Helena as a return to 'health'. In the same way that the renewed love of Oberon and Titania has brought harmony to the natural world so Demetrius says he has 'come to his natural taste' (172).

Theseus recognises the sincerity of Demetrius and allows the new sense of order that has emerged from the confusion in the wood to set aside the 'crime' of Lysander and Hermia. The play, however, continues to show how unreliable a concept 'reality' can be: each of the lovers attempts to define the experiences of the night and finds memory imprecise.

Bottom's awakening, though similar in some respects to the lovers' is one of the funniest and richest moments of the play. He, self-possessed as ever, needs no one to wake him and at first he seems still involved in rehearsals of 'Pyramus and Thisbe' but gradually the memory of his 'rare vision' steals over him. He hardly dares recall his transformation: three times he is on the brink of giving it words

> Methought I was – there is no man can tell what. Methought I was – and methought I had – (203-4)

each break in the dialogue is an invitation to the actor to let his hands hover over where his ass's head and ears have been. The sheer poetic grandeur of Bottom's dream is expressed first in his attempt to give it words and secondly in the punning title he wishes for it. He conveys his continuing sense of disorientation as he proclaims

> The eye of man hath not heard, the ear of man hath not seen, man's hand is not able to taste, his tongue to conceive, nor his heart to report what my dream was. (207-10)

and an Elizabethan audience would have recognised this as a confused misquotation of the Bible

> The eye hath not seen, and the ear hath not heard, neither have entered into the heart of man, the things which God hath prepared for them that love him. (I Corinthians, 2.9)

But the profundity of Bottom's dream is captured in the ballad which he hopes Peter Quince will write – profound because it 'hath no bottom' and yet very much *his*. In a flight of poetic fancy he imagines a performance 'before the Duke' in which his experience will be preserved – an occasion of great significance as befits a man who has been loved by and lost the

Queen of Fairies herself. As Bottom looks back on the night's events it is as if they have given him something that no one can take away.

Presiding over the whole scene, either by direct observance from the side of the stage, by presence on stage or by the extent of his influence, is Oberon. He has likened himself to a forester (III.ii.37) and his manipulation of events is like careful cultivation. In the final scene he will move into the mortal world to complete his work.

Act IV, Scene ii

Summary

The opening of this short scene shows us the rest of the Mechanicals. Back in Athens now, they are experiencing the sort of depression that all drama groups feel when someone is missing from rehearsal. They all agree that Bottom is quite irreplaceable. There is a very amusing moment when Quince (who should know better) uses the word 'paramour' (mistress) when he means 'paragon' and is quietly corrected by a very shocked Flute (who is obviously not so stupid as he seems).

Snug now enters with the news that there are to be even more noble weddings, simply increasing the sense of frustration. In a wonderful outburst, Flute seems inconsolable and convinced that 'sweet bully Bottom's' performance would have secured him a generous pension from Theseus.

Bottom now enters, his entrance almost as startling as when he last entered wearing his ass's head. We hear him coming, irrepressible as ever

> Where are these lads? Where are these hearts? (25)

and, typically, he has not wasted a moment. In the interval of time between this and the previous scene he has been to the palace and discovered that their play is chosen for the short list. Characteristically he interprets this to mean that their play is already selected for performance and he now takes command of the situation, handing out last-minute instructions to his delighted companions.

Commentary

This brief scene provides a breathing space in the action, enabling the audience to accept that a great deal happens between the previous scene in the wood and the following scene in court.

Act V

Summary

The stage represents Theseus's palace: the Duke and Hippolyta are discussing the events in the wood as told them by the lovers. Hippolyta is inclined to believe them but Theseus is sceptical and goes on to explain at some length the delusions which imagination can create.

With the entry of the four lovers we learn that the wedding ceremonies have already taken place – they exchange good wishes with Theseus who now calls upon Philostrate to say what entertainment is available to help pass the time till bedtime. The list contains various unappetising offerings and, of course, the workmen's play *Pyramus and Thisbe*. Attracted by its paradoxical description as 'tedious and brief', 'very tragical mirth', Theseus decides on seeing their performance in spite of Philostrate's insistence that the cast are incompetent amateurs and Hippolyta's distaste for seeing people undertaking what is beyond them. Theseus replies that it is people's intentions that matter most, and with a flourish of trumpets the play begins.

The performance is full of mistakes and inconsistencies and is punctuated by witty comments from the 'stage audience'. Theseus, however, thoroughly enjoys the entertainment and when the play ends Flute as Thisbe and Bottom as Pyramus lie 'dead', Bottom leaps up and offers an Epilogue or a Bergomask. Theseus chooses the latter and the workmen perform this peasant dance.

It is now midnight and Theseus says it is time for bed. When all the couples have left the stage Puck enters with a broom followed by Titania, Oberon and the Fairies who dance and sing – blessing the marriages, wishing them fruitful and protecting such offspring as there may be from disfigurement.

Puck is left alone on stage and asks for our applause, suggesting that the whole play might have been a dream.

Commentary

The scene falls naturally into four units: 1-27, 28-105, 106-362 and 363-429. Theseus's speech concerning the nature of the imagination (2-22) extends the themes touched on throughout the play. At first he seems dismissive of the whole concept of imagining, labelling the lovers' tales as 'antique fables and fairy toys' and equating lovers with madmen because their minds create more fantastic images than can ever be understood in the light of 'cool reason'. Imagination, Theseus reiterates at the end of the speech, belongs to darkness and night. He defends daylight and reality. Yet the audience knows the 'reality' of the events in which Hippolyta has a firm belief and when Theseus enlarges his list of those who depend on imagination to include poets the certainty of his case is undermined. What he intends as censure is interpreted by the audience as praise so that his cynicism is replaced by appreciation. This, in fact, is consistent with Theseus's behaviour throughout the play, for he frequently changes the tone of his speeches to reveal greater flexibility of mind than he seems to possess on the surface.

The lover, he says, sees exquisite beauty in a face whether it is really beautiful or not and the events of the play have demonstrated how the lover's eye can dote. The poet takes insubstantial ideas and gives them form: this is precisely what Shakespeare has done in creating a play and what actors do when they create living characters from a playwright's script. Ironically, Theseus cannot dismiss the power and importance of imagination because he himself is a character in a play: the drama can only exist if the audience agrees to *imagine* that the actor they are watching *is*, for the duration of the play, Theseus. The creative process whereby a person can personify a desired emotion (in his example, joy) is another fundamental aspect of drama (18-20) and there is an even greater irony to Theseus's description of the lover's experience as a combination of wish-fulfilment and delusions of darkness dismissed as 'antique fables'. What of Theseus's claim to 'reality'? Is he not a character from mythology with a very uncertain past?

Hippolyta reckons that the lovers' stories showed great consistency. The audience never hears the full account which the lovers give to Theseus and Hippolyta but 'these fairy toys' are obviously something which recollection and reflection have added, for whilst in the wood they were never aware of the Fairies and their influence. Significantly, Shakespeare gives Hipployta here (24) a word he uses in no other play: she speaks of their minds 'transfigured'. An Elizabethan audience would have been familiar with the New Testament event in which Christ revealed his essential divinity in a moment of transfiguration. Similarly, the lovers' minds are not simply changed by their experience, they are in some mysterious way made better.

Theseus's repeated wish of joy (29) to the two happy couples rings like wedding bells and, as at the opening of the play, he looks to live entertainment to make time pass quickly. The three hours which must elapse before bedtime are telescoped by Shakespeare with the same skill by which he has condensed the events of four days into a stage play of some three hours. Hippolyta's disinclination to see the amateur performance draws from Theseus a mild rebuke. In his wide travels Theseus has heard many attempts at speeches of homage by the most professional of orators. Overawed by the occasion, even they have stumbled over their words, yet Theseus has recognised genuine welcome and loyalty in what was said. This generous attitude of Theseus is generally taken as a tribute to the customary graciousness with which Queen Elizabeth accepted the faltering homage and entertainments provided by her subjects on her journeys (which were known as 'progresses') to stay at various houses and is a particularly apt prelude to the performance of *Pyramus and Thisbe*.

We shall be giving detailed consideration to *Pyramus and Thisbe* in a later section because the 'play within a play' sheds so much light on the theatrical conditions of the time in which it was written. There are, however, a number of points to be made here:

1. Shakespeare frequently used the device of an on-stage audience. Just as Oberon and Puck have been the audience watching the drama played out by the lovers, so, now, the lovers are the audience.
2. The play that they watch is a version of what *might* have happened to them had not Oberon intervened.
3. The lovers' comments, supposedly so rational, witty and sophisticated, are ironic in the light of their earlier conduct.
4. *Pyramus and Thisbe* is *much* funnier in performance than on the page: some of the humour derives from (a) the efforts of the amateurs to speak verse; (b) the failure of that verse to cope with the high emotions it tries to express; (c) the incongruity of the acting performances and of the personification of wall, lion and moonshine; (d) the seriousness with which the performance is undertaken. Note, for example, the wonderful moment when Bottom comes out of role to explain to Theseus the action of the play:

   > No, in truth, sir, he should not. 'Deceiving me' is Thisbe's cue. She is to enter now, and I am to spy her through the wall. You shall see – it will fall pat as I told you.   (181-4)

   and note the humorous interchanges between Theseus, the lovers and the performers which are heightened by the Mechanicals' intense concentration; (e) the play itself is a parody of some contemporary forms of drama. Obviously this aspect and some of the jokes of the spectators are much more difficult for a modern audience to appreciate.
5. Theseus is always kind and courteous to the actors and remains engrossed in their performance throughout. We share his enjoyment. Note how he stresses the need for the audience to use *their* imagination and his reference to actors as 'shadows' – one of Shakespeare's favourite descriptions of actors. Compare this with the first line of Puck's final speech of the play in which he employs the word 'shadows' to have the double meaning of spirits and actors (compare 208 and 414).
6. Hippolyta shows very little generosity or imagination in her attitude towards the performance and consequently derives little enjoyment from it. See lines 208 and 245.
7. Even Theseus prefers not to see the epilogue and rounds off the entertainment with a dance – this is the second time that a dance is used as a harmonious conclusion to events (compare IV.i.84).

As always when he is on stage, Theseus has the last word as he acknowledges that it is now past midnight when the Fairies, once again, take control and he urges all the company to retire to their marriage beds. The waiting for this moment, which Theseus has referred to in the opening lines of the play, is now over and his final words re-echo those of his first appearance when he called for celebration and festivity.

The final moments of *A Midsummer Night's Dream* are a magical, stately and subtle blend of formality and apparent spontaneity. Puck first creates the atmosphere when he appears on the empty stage. His speech (363-82) conjures up images of the mystery of night as opposed to the rational daylight by describing the disturbing sounds of the darkness – the hungry lion roaring, the wolf howling at the moon, the owl screeching – while the exhausted labourer snores and the embers glow in the hearth. Night, he says, also releases spirits of death and these will haunt those who go to bed 'in woe'; Puck creates a sense of ghostly movement as he talks of the phantoms leaving their graves in the churchyard and of Hecate's horse-drawn chariot moving away from the sun. The whole atmosphere of the central portion of the play is restated in Puck's phrase 'following darkness like a dream' but he also re-emphasises that the Fairies are not part of the evil associations of the night. He has come in his traditional 'broom-carrying' role to 'sweep the dust behind the door', symbolising his bringing of well-being and peace to 'this hallowed house'.

When the entire Fairy court occupies the palace they perform almost a tiny masque to seal the harmony of the relationships and celebrate the sanctity of marriage. Fairies move to every corner of the house, Oberon and Titania going significantly to the bedroom of Theseus and Hippolyta to wish blessing on the lovers now eternally joined. These marriages will remain harmonious and the children born to the couples will have none of Nature's imperfections – we have already seen how conflict in the love of Oberon and Titania has brought about the disturbance of Nature but no such unnaturalness will be the outcome of further marital strife.

Finally Puck speaks directly to the audience – he suggests that if the 'shadows' have offended then the audience should think of it all as a dream. Puck expresses beautifully something of what poor Quince was trying to say in the Prologue to *Pyramus and Thisbe*, and he exploits the dual meaning of shadow to underline the dream-like quality of not only this particular play but of drama in general. A play is ephemeral, insubstantial and when ended the actors who have (as Theseus put it) 'beguiled the time' invite our applause.

3 THEMES AND ISSUES

3.1 LOVE AND MARRIAGE

Shakespeare presents so many aspects of love and its effects in this play that it is impossible to single out a particularly dominant view. The characters, the actions and the images all make 'statements' about love, some of which have almost become clichés, and it is only by considering many of these that we can begin to understand the dramatist's thinking. First, we should distinguish between the love *through the senses* which Shakespeare calls 'doting' and the more permanent kind of love, which the play ultimately seems to advocate, in which there is an element of *mind*. This is not to underestimate Shakespeare's attitude to the physical aspects of love for the play begins with a couple impatient for their wedding and ends with three couples about to legitimately consummate their love in bed. However, when love is nothing more than a doting through the senses it becomes a fixation lacking reason and this is presented very clearly in the memorable visual image of Titania making love to the ass-headed Bottom.

The lack of reason in love has been suggested by some critics as a dominant theme in the play and Bottom's statement that 'reason and love keep little company' could be seen as confirming the irrationality of love. But if we look closer at the play we find that not only does love not depend on reason alone but that this is a source of its strength and wonder. It is true that under the influence of the love juice the young lovers behave strangely, yet in the end they return to their first romantic attachments and this is far more than a simple triumph of reason. The relationship between Theseus and Hippolyta, which Shakespeare presents as the most stable in the play is certainly a *blend* of passion and thought, and the 'reasoning' which Theseus urges on Hermia in the opening scene does nothing to change her love for Lysander.

A Midsummer Night's Dream celebrates marriage as the proper outcome of true love. Egeus, of course, believes in 'arranged marriages' but ultimately Theseus sees that the genuine love of a young couple is more important than a father's wishes. Enforced chastity is shown as something sterile and unnatural (see I.i.70-6) but this must be contrasted with the freedom and nobility of *elected* chastity, typified by the image of the virgin queen, Elizabeth.

The status and permanence which Shakespeare gives to marriage makes its breakdown all the more painful and the rift between Oberon and Titania is so serious a reversal of the natural state that it is reflected in the larger natural world. Impediments to the free flow of love and loyalty between couples are presented in nightmarish terms – Hermia wakes from a dream about a serpent to find Lysander gone, the wall which separates Pyramus and Thisby is 'vile', and Demistrius's jilting of Helena forces her to behave in uncharacteristic ways. In the list which follows I have indicated some of the play's statements about love, all of which are, perhaps, summed up in the most famous line 'The course of true love never did run smooth' (I.i.134).

	Reference examples
Love is painful.	I.i.128–55, 226, 250; II.i.213, 243
Love is blind.	I.i.235; III.i.147; V.i.4–11
Lovers *think* they are rational.	III.ii.134
Love seems to have no alternative but hate.	II.ii.141–8
Love can be absurd.	See all the statements made by Lysander and Demetrius after the 'love juice' – and Titania's scenes with Bottom.
Love is like madness.	II.ii.192; III.ii.450–1
Love must have freedom to flourish but must be the basis of society.	Consider Hermia and Lysander's need to escape but the evenual culmination of the play in three marriages.
Love is often the subject of young women's 'private' conversations.	I.i.214–6
Love enables people to understand each other more fully.	II.ii.52
True, permanent love, is a state of happiness.	V.i.399

You should find more examples under these headings *and* provide further statements from the play. It is vital that this be done in conjunction with the later section on 'Imagery' (where I have discussed the ideas of Cupid versus Diana) and bearing in mind the tensions caused by parental interference in love affairs and the possible tragic outcome of love which is parodied in *Pyramus and Thisbe*. We must remember that the same idea lies behind *Romeo and Juliet* - Shakespeare's most poignant tragedy on the subject of young love. To some extent the playwright seems to be saying in *A Midsummer Night's Dream* that wisdom in these matters comes with age; Theseus certainly has greater control and balance than the 'young lovers' - but Lysander and Hermia, in order to consummate their true love, have to escape the wishes of Egeus and follow their own destiny. Both Theseus and Hippolyta are, if we are to believe the Fairies, experienced lovers and it may be not be so much *age* as *suffering*, such as the night in the wood brings to the four young people, that teaches. Egeus, though an older man, is certainly not portrayed as wise and neither Titania nor Oberon, who are not governed by a mortal timespan, is able to avoid a rift in their love. Indeed Shakespeare makes us realise that the very existence of deep love between two beings makes them vulnerable to conflict.

3.2 DISCORD AND CONCORD

We have noted this theme in the commentary on the scenes and later in the section on 'Music and Dancing', and they should need little amplification at this point because you should look for your own examples. The play abounds in contrasts which underline these opposites: the darkness of the wood and the daylight of Athens; the chaos of the lovers' actions and the resolution in marriage; the disorderly barking of the hounds producing 'music'; the 'Mechanicals' play which is both comedy and tragedy, and so on. Each relationship in the play passes through a phase of discord before its final harmony: Theseus has been at war with Hippolyta before wooing her; Egeus is at odds with Hermia; Lysander and Hermia are temporarily in conflict - and so the pattern repeats itself throughout the action. The most powerful image of discord is that of the terrible weather which has resulted from Oberon and Titania's quarrel; in this situation things have become *unnatural*, for discord is contrary to the purposes of nature. In human terms the only remedy is reconciliation, a favourite theme of Shakespeare's comedies, and in this play the happy end is brought about by Oberon, representing benign providence.

3.3 IMAGINATION

Without imagination there can be no drama. Theseus makes this quite clear in Act V when he patiently explains to Hippolyta that imagination is necessary if the actor's work is to be understood (210). Hippolyta is rather slow on the uptake at this juncture and retorts 'It must be your imagination then, and not theirs' (211) which is *precisely* the point Theseus has been making, although he would not deny that the actor *does need* imagination. In their discussion of the need for walls, lions and moonlight the Mechanicals have groped towards an understanding of the need for audience imagination at the performance of their play but they never really come to terms with the potential *power* of this wonderful human attribute.

Love, fear and other emotions all feed the imagination. Titania *thinks* she hears and sees beauty in Bottom; Demetrius and Lysander *imagine* that each of the two girls is more attractive than the other. Theseus sums it up

> The lover, all as frantic,
> Sees Helen's beauty in a brow of Egypt.   (V.i.10–11)

or, as Helena observes

> Things base and vile, holding no quantity,
> Love can transpose to form and dignity.   (I.i.232–3)

The fear of losing Lysander leads Hermia to imagine that Demetrius has killed him: the fierce jealousy of Oberon and Titania causes each to imagine that the other has been having an affair with Hippolyta or Theseus: the anxieties of each of these characters is such that imagination takes an idea or a small hint and turns it into evidence.

It is imagination that brings humans nearest to god-like status for by its power they create something out of nothing. Things that are insubstantial are given form and shape; connections are made between apparently disparate elements. Theseus understands this and summarises the potency of imagination in his famous speech at the opening of Act V. The speech (which is discussed in the appropriate scene commentary) dwells on the dangers as well as the achievements of the imagination, and culminates by considering the poet (and playwright). Again we see a need for *balance*; to be composed entirely of imagination as the lunatic, the lover and the poet tend to be, may lead to a type of blindness.

3.4 DREAMS, ILLUSIONS AND REALITY

Such is the power of imagination that its products may seem more 'real' than reality itself – as we see on the stage. Indeed, the margins between reality and imagination are often so vague that they seem to disappear altogether. This is the experience of the four lovers as they awake from the sleep into which Puck has led them.

DEMETRIUS   These things seem small and undistinguishable,
                   Like far-off mountains turned into clouds.

HERMIA   Methinks I see these things with parted eye,
               When everything seems double.   (IV.i.183–6)

Several characters have dreams in the course of the play; Hermia, with Lysander a short distance from her, sinks exhausted to sleep but has a nightmare in which a serpent is crawling over her breast (II.ii.151–6). When she wakes the dream becomes reality. Titania's love affair with Bottom is entirely 'real' to both characters and we, the audience, watch its progress. Yet when they are both awake they are unable to articulate their experience and doubt its reality. It is as if they find their behaviour so incredible and can only come to terms with it if they assume that they have been dreaming. Oberon (III.ii.377–8) provides the same solution to the four lovers by ensuring that they will all look back on the night's events as figments of the imagination. As we have seen, they feel that sense of confusion typical of waking but they also go on to question just what *was* real, and, as they find certain points of agreement, may privately think that they have been *awake* but each suffering from an illusion (see IV.i. 190–7). Some of the sense of unreality in this play is also the result of the strange combination of Fairies, Elizabethan lovers and artisans and mythological Grecians.

Perhaps the supreme example of illusion is drama itself. The actors and actresses are *themselves* yet pretend to be *other people*, and we accept them as such. The place *is* the stage, yet it represents somewhere else. Time *is* that moment when the play takes place, but is accepted as being another time; time is also shaped, so that three hours may be represented twenty minutes, or three days by three hours. Quince and his cast find the nature of dramatic illusion hard to grasp; they worry about the audience thinking that the actor playing Pyramus has really killed himself or that the 'lion' is a 'real' lion.

Shakespeare is always aware of the doubtful 'reality' of a play. He uses the term shadows to describe actors, and how 'real' is a shadow? In Puck's final speech the playwright seems to be playing the ultimate trick on us by suggesting that, perhaps, the whole play was a dream and we have been sleeping all the while. But there is a truth in the play which gives his imaginative work a very special quality.

4 TECHNIQUES

4.1 CHARACTERS AND CHARACTERISATION

It is only possible to say anything of value about the characters in a play when their words, actions and motives have been thoroughly examined. It is a good idea to try reading the scenes through from the point of view of *each* of the characters in turn, considering not only what they say but also what they are doing when they are *not* speaking. This will provide insights into what actors call the 'subtext' – the drives and concerns which lie beneath what a character says.

A Midsummer Night's Dream is sometimes thought to be 'weak' in the area of characterisation. It is true that the play provides no penetrating psychological study of a human being such as we find in *Macbeth* or *King Lear* but that is to judge the play by the wrong criteria. The interest lies in the situations, ideas, images, atmosphere and spectacle: the characters sustain all of these rather than providing profound revelations of themselves. Nevertheless, the text does give the actor a considerable number of clues for the creation of believable and fascinating characters and these we must now examine.

Theseus
Theseus is the pivot of the entire play. It is his triumph over the Amazon queen and his approaching marriage to her that provides its timespan, that has brought Oberon and Titania to the woods near Athens and that has provided a reason for the 'Mechanicals' to rehease and perform their play. It is Theseus's judgement that gives the young lovers a reason and an opportunity to enter the woods and it is his decision which finally resolves the conflict. Of the mortals in the play he has the first word and the last; he is a sportsman, a patron of the arts and a benevolent ruler.

The first thing an actor playing Theseus will notice is that when he is on stage he speaks a great many lines. He certainly dominates the scenes both in terms of his presence and his language. This is entirely appropriate for a figure of authority who represents government and law, and Theseus uses the elaborate speech with which these are associated. Theseus rather likes the sound of his own voice but much of his talking derives from his patience and kindness. Although he is impatient for his marriage he listens with great care to the case brought before him by Egeus and is similarly patient in his explanations of the need for imagination and understanding to Hippolyta. In the opening scene he is remarkably tolerant of Hermia's sharp, possibly defiant replies and his 'In himself he is' (line 53) is a reasonable and restrained answer. He urges patience on the headstrong young lovers and shows himself prepared to listen to reason. While he appears unbending in his attitude to the law in the opening scene, we never know what 'private schooling' he offers to Egeus and Demetrius and he is remarkably quick to overturn the letter of the law when he sees that it runs counter to the wishes of the four lovers and to common sense.

Theseus in some respects epitomises common sense and reason, yet he is a pleasure-loving duke with an almost scandalous past. His amorous adventures are, however, almost glossed over by Shakespeare and as they are mentioned only in the jealous confrontation of Oberon and Titania, may even be discounted altogether. At his first and last appearances in the play he announces periods of revelry and entertainment, he greatly enjoys hunting and he is the only member of the court to be engrossed in the 'Mechanicals'' play, enjoying every moment for what it is. Shakespeare has taken this hero-figure whose exploits he may have read about in Plutarch's *Lives* or Chaucer's *Knight's Tale* and used his exotic adventures as a background for his involvement with the immortals. His headstrong and passionate youth enables him to offer understanding to the lovers, and his final love for Hippolyta, to whom he is very attentive throughout the play, makes him particularly sensitive to the culmination of love in his marriage.

Theseus takes his state duties seriously, he enjoys solemn ceremony which symbolises order and harmony and, like Queen Elizabeth I, he finds pleasure in the loyalty of the lowliest of all his subjects. Fortunately he combined these qualities with a sense of humour.

Hippolyta
Hippolyta is a somewhat colourless character. She takes no part in the affairs of state and rarely speaks. Her role as a former warrior queen of great beauty is only hinted at in Titania's savage remarks to Oberon, but we do see evidence of her 'bouncing' physique and her fame as a huntress in her enthusiastic participation in Theseus's hunt. Although she is prepared to give more credence to the lovers' tale of their exploits in the wood than is Theseus, Hippolyta generally seems to lack imagination.

Her reaction to the plight of Hermia in the opening scene may be sympathetic but otherwise she seems faintly bored in most of her appearances on stage; her remarks concerning *Pyramus and Thisbe*, which she finds tiresome, are cutting and never witty. Yet Hippolyta is important in providing an image of mature love as a contrast to the headstrong 'young love' and, as we shall see in the section on imagery, her association with Diana, the huntress and goddess of the moon, is very significant.

Lysander

Lysander, like all the other lovers, comes from no obvious source except the tradition of Elizabethan courtly poetry. He is the most forthright of the lovers (think of his impertinent remark to Egeus) and his language is impressive and beautiful until his transformation in II.ii.109. He mounts a powerful argument in I.i and then shows great tenderness towards Hermia; he even retains enough sensitivity to realise that Demetrius is behaving unkindly in III.ii.160.

Lysander issues a challenge to Demetrius whereas Demetrius has simply made vague threats; his rudeness and cruelty to Hermia under the influence of the love juice are outrageous and he tends to be the spokesman for the lovers: both when they wake in IV.i and when they enter in V.i.30 he is the first to speak and he is the first lover to make an witty comment during the 'Mechanicals'' play (V.i.119). His ironic 'proceed Moon' is the most self-confident of all the lovers' remarks.

We must remember that audience sympathy tends to be with Lysander at the opening of the play and we continue to judge him in that light. Perhaps the most interesting feature of his character is that he is the one lover who says nothing about his recollections of the night's events; he certainly has the most to be ashamed of.

Demetrius

Critics of the play have sometimes remarked that the characterisation of the lovers is so 'thin' that they are virtually interchangeable. This is only true insofar as they show a similar pattern of behaviour in love and their obsession prevents our discovering more about them. Both Lysander and Demetrius appear to be wealthy Athenians, although Lysander claims (I.i.102) to be slightly better endowed. Demetrius is the first of the men to speak before Theseus but he quickly loses all audience sympathy once his former love for Helena is revealed. The next time we see him he is in a rage and intent on doing violence to Lysander (II.i.190). He is already suffering a kind of madness – 'wood within this wood' and is completely at a loss to know how to be rid of Helena. Demetrius is *always* in an uncomfortable position (see III.ii.59); no sooner has he found Hermia than he is being accused of Lysander's murder. No doubt this is why he constantly resorts to threats both to Helena and Lysander as a way of coping with his tension. Demetrius is the only character in the play to remain under the spell of the love juice and it is he who gives the most graphic account of the sensation of waking from the 'dream'. In his case, of course, the boundaries between 'dream' and 'reality' are even more indeterminate (IV.i.191).

Hermia

There is some speculation that the physically contrasting figures of Hermia and Helena were incorporated into this play because Shakespeare had a tall, fair boy and a short, dark boy in his company at the time. Certainly there are many references to Hermia's small stature and dark complexion, indeed the insulting comments of Lysander suggest she is *very* dark. We must remember that in Shakespeare's day very dark women were generally considered less attractive than fair women. This makes Hermia's position more vulnerable and we can expect her to be particularly sensitive to comments about her dark appearance.

Hermia is the most consistent of the lovers; she is utterly loyal and never wavers in her love for Lysander. She is entirely the victim of circumstances and none of the problems she encounters can be said to be of her own making. From her first words in the play we find her determined and fiery. She is easily moved; we see her on the verge of tears and she reveals an aggressive temper; we learn from Helena that she was like this as a schoolgirl but the two women have remained close friends since that time. Foolishly, perhaps, the habit they have developed of telling each other *everything* is taken too far by Hermia in her revelation of the escape plan, though it is actually Lysander who begins to reveal the scheme to Helena.

Hermia probably captures the sympathy of the audience from the first: she has a difficult and interfering father; she shows considerable courage in her defiance of him; she demonstrates restraint and decorum in her refusal to sleep beside Lysander and it is easy to understand her impassioned outbursts (for example, in III.ii.65) as her situation becomes even more intolerable.

Helena

A certain amount of humour derives from the difference in height between the two women and it is appropriate that Helena's long legs are the subject of several jokes because she spends much of her time chasing or running away. Helena seems to understand the problems of love as shown in her long speech in I.i.226-51, but is powerless to do anything about it. Such is the effect of love on her that she finds that it drives her to break the trust of her best friend and to end up in a situation where she occupies what traditionally has been a man's role (see II.i.240-2).

Helena is sometimes portrayed as a rather foolish, fawning character, throwing herself at the feet of Demetrius and complaining when he treads on her. In her reaction to the sudden reversal of the situation and the behaviour of Hermia she seems cowardly and timid. But we must remember that Helena has been jilted before the start of the play and, to make matters worse, her lover has transferred his affection to her best friend. We can, therefore, appreciate her dilemma and it is not surprising that she finds her loyalty to her friend Hermia strained by jealousy, if not suspicion. She is, in fact, the more conventionally feminine of the two young women, finding it distasteful to try to woo Demetrius because she feels that it is women's role to be wooed. Because she has been jilted she has lost confidence in herself and thinks herself ugly but when it comes to an argument with Hermia she knows where her rival is vulnerable and scores some devastating points in their quarrel. It is difficult not to find Helena's entrance in III.ii.441 extremely moving and her role throughout the play as the jilted lover desperately trying to find a way back into favour is one of Shakespeare's most delicate touches.

Oberon

Shakespeare probably took the idea of Oberon from the old romance *Huon of Bordeaux* and he clearly links him with the figure of 'the Lord of Misrule' who presided over traditional 'Maying' revels. Just as Theseus dictates events in the court of Athens so Oberon is the pivot of the action in the wood. His authority, in fact, extends into Theseus's world and we see him bringing his blessing to mortal marriage in the final scene of the play.

Oberon inhabits dreams; his activities are exotic and removed from human experience and he recounts how he

>   sat upon a promontory
> And heard a mermaid on a dolphin's back
> Uttering such dulcet and harmonious breath
> That the rude sea grew civil at her song,
> And certain stars shot madly from their spheres
> To hear the sea-maid's music. (II.1.149-54)

He says that he has 'with the morning's love... oft made sport' and that only he could see Cupid's arrow as it shot from the bow. As he remarks to Puck, 'We are spirits of another sort' (III.ii.395) and he demonstrates his 'otherness' in the richness, beauty and magnificence of the lines he speaks.

Oberon enjoys considerable supernatural power; he can make himself invisible and knows the magical properties of the flowers and herbs, he can upset and bring harmony to nature and is impatient when his will is thwarted. When we first meet this 'king of shadows' he seems imperious and vindictive; we never fully understand precisely why he wants the Indian boy but he seems prepared to go to great lengths to achieve his ends. It is as if the flouting of his authority rather than the actual *need* for the boy is what drives him and he shows little tolerance to Puck when his orders are apparently disobeyed. Nevertheless, it is with *pity* and compassion that we come to associate Oberon – he is moved by the plight of Helena and eventually by that of Titania. He is concerned that his Queen's affection for the Indian boy has become a fixation which is damaging her perception and their relationship. Oberon acts as a benign force towards the other characters in the play and solves the problems they cannot handle themselves.

Puck

Puck is the Robin Goodfellow of English folklore. His natural habitat is darkness and he twice refers to the approach of morning as if it marked the diminution of his powers (see III.ii.385 and IV.i.91). He is capable of bringing darkness, as we see when Oberon orders him to 'overcast the night' in II.ii, and he seems happiest when he is causing confusion. Of all the Fairies he is the one who brings us closest to the dark side of the supernatural world; his speeches in III.ii.387-94 and V.i.363-82 are full of references to unhappy, damned spirits but his actual manifestations of evil are confined to practical jokes. It is important to notice, however, that Oberon's statement 'We are spirits of another sort' *also* refers to Puck and follows straight after Puck's speech about 'damned spirits' (III.ii.389-94); This is a clear indication that Puck is not associated with *evil* so much, perhaps, as with error, fear and superstition emanating from the unknown. Puck is Oberon's jester whose sense of fun is provoked by the distress of mankind. He is not, however, a clown and we do not laugh *at* him so much as *with* him and at the results of his actions. At times he is the 'audience' on stage, passing comment on the stupidity of humans with whom he is more closely involved than any of the Fairies. Some of the events of the play are made possible by his incredible powers – he can 'put a girdle round the earth in forty minutes' and travel faster than an 'arrow from the Tartar's bow', He can change his appearance and his voice at will but under Oberon's authority even he seems pleased when the 'jangling' in the wood is resolved.

Puck's contribution to the action of the play is considerable: his mistaken identification of the lovers and his interference in the 'mechanicals' bring about the most fascinating and comic twists to the plot. It is he who fetches the love juice and leads the lovers in their final desperate chase. He is very much a performer, pausing to ask Oberon and us to watch – 'I go, I go – look how I go –' (III.ii.100) and inviting our applause at the end of the play.

Bottom
Puck is particularly severe on Bottom, whom he considers to be 'The shallowest thickskin of that barren sort' (III.ii.13) and removes his ass's head with the words 'Now, when thou wak'st, with thine own fool's eyes peep (IV.1.82). Yet most members of an audience would view Bottom with far greater sympathy and affection; he is truly one of Shakespeare's most memorable creations. There is, indeed, a good deal of significance in Bottom's description of his experience as 'Bottom's Dream' for that might well be the title of Shakespeare's play.

Bottom (whose name is not just a crude pun on arse and ass but is also taken from the reel onto which a weaver wound his thread) is the undisputed leader of the group of 'Mechanicals' in spite of Quince's nominal authority. He is obviously a friend of Quince's and likes to give the impression that he has read his play before Quince introduces it to the rest of the cast. He is not so much an actor as a 'stand-up comic', a clown who relates directly to his audience and wants to put on a one-man show, hence his desire to play *all* the parts in the play. Bottom also has a gift for language and his constant misuse of long words is only partly a sign of ignorance whereas the restricted vocabulary of his friends is precisely that; it is a reaching out towards a poetic world of imagination on Bottom's part and an escape from the mundane, everyday world of the manual worker.

It is Bottom's imaginative flair that enables him to cope with the most horrific transformation. For all his lack of sophistication he never loses his extraordinary self-possession, he remains perfectly aware that he is neither 'wise' nor 'beautiful' but adapts far better than anyone else in the play to a role in which he finds himself the object of almost unlimited passion. He jokes about his hairy face and his appetite for oats and dried peas whilst holding court among the Fairies, even understanding their involvement in nature, with all the gentleness of Gulliver in Lilliput in Jonathan Swift's *Gulliver's Travels*.

Bottom's friends recognise his qualities; they know that without him they simply cannot go on and that it will be he who will attract attention by his performance (see IV.ii). They all, especially Flute, regard him with great affection. This is hardly surprising for although he is very self-centred he is never objectionable. He does have some knowledge of plays and acting and his enthusiasm and love for the theatre make him an amateur in the true sense. He has a genuine stage presence, he never makes a dull entrance and once he starts to pose questions about the mystery of theatre, as he does in Act III, he answers them all himself!

This resourceful figure, who totally dominates the scene when he is on stage, is funny because we can laugh at him and with him in total sympathy. The ease with which Quince convinces him he must play Pyramus by a little flattery; the wonderful exchange with the 'audience' as he lies dead in *Pyramus and Thisbe*; the comic timing in his 'awaking' speech are superb examples of humorous writing for the stage. But Bottom's function in the play is not purely comical: he may be the play's most memorable fool but in recognising that 'reason and love keep little company nowadays' he speaks more sense than the educated and sophisticated. He provides an essential link between the mortals and the Fairy world by his involvement with Titania and is the means whereby Oberon cures his queen of her obsession – he is an even more ridiculous fixation than the Indian boy once he has acquired his ass head. In Bottom the frontier between 'performing' (which he enjoys) and behaving normally is very vague and this further enriches the ideas of appearance and reality with which the play deals.

Titania

From Titania's initial meeting with Oberon we gain the impression of a resolute personality unwilling to give in to persuasion. Her concern for the Indian boy is a product of her love for the boy's mother and this seems to be typical of her attitude towards humans for she seems genuinely concerned that her quarrel with Oberon has brought hardship to mankind, and her involvement with Bottom is by far the most intimate in the play.

Titania inhabits a world of dancing, music and flowers, a world of sensuousness and beauty. Her concept of pleasure is to lie among scented flowers and she reveals a most passionate nature once she falls in love with Bottom. Her delicacy and lightness contrast with the 'mortal grossness' of Bottom and it is perhaps surprising that Oberon's taunts change her mind about the custody of the child. Her concern for the boy has, however, grown out of all proportion – a point that was brought home powerfully in a recent BBC Television production when the tiny boy was clasped to Titania's bosom from the moment of her first appearance until she is lulled asleep. Accordingly she has become unattentive and disloyal to Oberon and must be corrected. The renewal of her love for Oberon brings deeper happiness to both of them.

4.2 THE LANGUAGE

The words spoken by various characters and a few stage directions are the only elements which a playwright leaves us for the creation of his play. Language, therefore, has many functions in a playtext: it may provide essential information for the context of the play; it provides insights into the minds of the characters; it evokes mental images in the imaginations of the audience; it differentiates between the characters and it must be accepted by the audience as representing 'real' dialogue spoken by believable people.

Shakespeare's mastery of dramatic language is clearly demonstrated in *A Midsummer Night's Dream.* As in all his plays, he mainly wrote in verse and it has been said that he never wrote better poetry than in this play. This may be true but we must remember that the poetry never ceases to be functional in furthering the action of the play. The metrical structure, rhyme-scheme, the introduction of prose and its juxtaposition with verse all serve a dramatic purpose.

Each style of language establishes the 'world' which its speakers inhabit and Shakespeare's manipulation of these worlds is achieved through the incredible *variety* of language he employs within a single play. This variety stems not only from different metrical structures but also from a rich and colourful vocabulary. The detail and beauty of the natural world is evoked by Shakespeare's careful choice of words: Lysander speaks of Phoebe, the moon, 'Decking with liquid pearl the bladed grass', each word, particularly the adjectives 'liquid' and 'bladed' contributing a new dimension to the total image because of their accuracy and delicacy. Similarly Hermia talks of '*faint* primrose beds', a wonderful way of evoking both colour and scent, Titania speaks of '*hoary-headed* frosts' and Oberon of '*nodding* violets'. The same technique is employed by Titania to describe the more violent aspects of nature when she speaks of 'the *whistling* wind', '*contagious* fogs' and 'every *pelting* river'. In addition to the recurrent images of the play, such as the moon and flowers (which we examine in detail in the next section) Shakespeare uses his vocabulary to create striking images throughout the play, often in the form of *similes.* Helena says that she and Hermia were 'like two artificial gods' and 'like to a double cherry', Oberon says he was 'like a forester'; Demetrius describes his thought on waking as 'like far-off mountains', Helena says she has found Demetrius 'like a jewel' and so on.

As we shall see in our section on '*A Midsummer Night's Dream* in the Theatre', it is Shakespeare's vocabulary which so often creates the atmosphere of the play and enriches the imagination of the audience so that the ear stimulates both the eye and even the sense of smell in the mind. Notice how the words '*spiced* Indian air', '*sweet* musk roses', '*drooping* fog', 'this *cold* bed' work on our senses to create a total world on Shakespeare's bare stage.

4.3 RHYME AND RHYTHM

The basic Shakespearean line is of ten syllables: a decasyllabic line; and is unrhymed. This 'blank verse' line is normally an 'iambic pentameter', that is a line of ten syllables divided into five 'feet' each of which is an iamb consisting of an unstressed syllable ($\cup$) followed by a stressed syllable ($-$). The lines are designed to be spoken so that the natural stresses of everyday speech provide the rhythm, for example

> The ox hath therefore stretched his yoke in vain
> $\cup\ -\ |\ \cup\ -\ |\ \cup\ -\ |\ \cup\ -\ |\ \cup\ -\ |$

Sometimes a line will be divided between two speakers but its rhythmic structure remains the same, for example

OBERON: I do but beg a little changeling boy
to be my henchman.
$\cup\ -\ |\ \cup\ -\ |\ \cup$

TITANIA: Set your heart at rest:
$-\ |\ \cup\ -\ |\ \cup\ -\ |$

The fairy land buys not the child of me.

In this example Shakespeare has actually split the iamb between the characters!

Obviously a play consisting entirely of iambic pentameters would become very tedious and some of the verse in *Pyramus and Thisbe* clearly parodies the way in which natural speech rhythm would have to be contorted to fit so inflexible a pattern. Shakespeare, therefore, makes several variations in his basic line. Instead of the iamb he sometimes uses the trochee, which is the exact reverse of the iamb, thus $-\ \cup$, and he also introduces feet consisting of two unstressed syllables followed by a stressed: $\cup\cup -$ (the anapaest), the reverse of that: $-\ \cup\cup$ (the dactyl) and two stressed syllables together (the spondee) $-\ -$, or two unstressed syllables together (the dibrach) $\cup\ \cup$. Where one type of foot is replaced by its exact opposite we usually speak of 'inversion' and where the basic foot (in this case the iamb) is replaced by another we refer to 'substitution'.

Here are some examples from the play

> Four days will quickly steep themselves in night
> $-\ -\ |\ \cup\ -\ |\ \cup\ -\ |\ \cup\ -\ |\ \cup\ -\ |$

> And then the moon like to a silver bow
> $\cup\ -\ |\ \cup\ |\ -\ |\ -\ \cup\cup\ |\ -\ \cup\ |\ -$

Stir up the Athenian youth to merriments

Such variations in metre, together with the fact that very few lines are 'end stopped', most continuing their sense into the following line, provide for a natural flow and energy in the verse. In *A Midsummer Night's Dream*, however, Shakespeare achieves a quite remarkable degree of variety in the verse by the introduction of rhyme and of some lines of completely different length.

In I.i.171 Hermia begins to speak in rhymed pentameters and this style is picked up by Lysander and Helena for the rest of the scene. The lines rhyme in pairs and dialogue in 'rhyming couplets' has a very distinctive and attractive quality; it is, in fact, the basic dialogue structure now used for 'traditional' pantomime and it can give a sense of unreality, absurdity, artificiality and rapid exchange. The same rhyme scheme is used by Puck and the Fairy in Act II, but the entry of Oberon and Titania signals a return to blank verse – they have far weightier matters to deal with and their elevated language befits their roles.

When Demetrius and Helena appear in II.i.188 they are in a strange state of turmoil which is reflected in an erratic rhyme scheme before they finally return to blank verse. But the rhyming couplets (with a brief variation into a, b, a b,) are reintroduced with the entry of Hermia and Lysander (II.ii.41) and are retained for the ludicrous exchange between Helena and Demetrius (line 89), Lysander's awakening and Hermia's final distress. As if the magic powers of the wood have worked on her too, Titania speaks in rhyme when she falls in love with Bottom (III.i.151) and this contrasts humorously with the crude verse of Bottom's song and with the prose in which he speaks. Titania's rhyming becomes even more insistent as she falls deeper in love and at one point the rhymes are regularly repeated

> Hop in his walks and gambol in his eyes;
> Feed him with apricocks and dewberries,
> With purple grapes, green figs, and mulberries.
> The honey-bags steal from the humble-bees,
> And for night-tapers crop their waxen thighs,
> And light them at the fiery glow-worm's eyes
> To have my love to bed and to arise,
> And pluck the wings from painted butterflies
> To fan the moonbeams from his sleeping eyes   (II.i.168–76)

Rhyming couplets are used by Puck to tell Oberon of Titania's amusing situation and for Oberon's delighted response (III.ii.6 onward); Hermia and Demetrius continue to speak in this way as Puck and Oberon watch them and then Puck and Oberon converse similarly. When lovers reappear, however, at line 122 in the same scene they use an a, b, a, b, rhyme scheme which suits their heated interchanges. This is then replaced by rhyming couplets as Demetrius wakes to make his highly artificial declaration of love for Helena. Rhyme continues until, at line 196, it is replaced by blank verse for the rest of the scene, thus enabling the more genuine emotions to be conveyed and the scene to change pace. A half-rhyme scheme is used for the confused pursuit of Lysander and Demetrius but each lover speaks in rhyme as they are brought to sleep by Puck, and it is interesting to note that even at this point Shakespeare gives each lover a distinctive rhyme patterns (see III.ii.422-56). The lovers never converse in rhyme again and in the daylight world of the court they speak only rational, if rather trite, prose.

The effect of rhyming verse is often to give language a sense of decorativeness and magic. This is certainly the case with Oberon's exquisite description of Titania's bower (II.ii.249-59), the remaining lines of that scene and the superb words of Puck and Oberon (III.ii.35 onwards) in which they express a deep affinity with the mysterious powers of the universe. An even more intriguing variation of Shakespeare's verse is the rhymed lines of seven syllables with which Oberon and Puck exercise magic power: examples of this simple but haunting and incantatory language occur in II.ii when Oberon squeezes love juice into Titania's eyes, again when Puck squeezes juice into Lysander's eyes and in III.ii when Oberon does the same to Demetrius. Puck's 'up and down' speech in III.ii, his spell on the four lovers, Oberon's words to awake Titania, her conversation after their dance and the entire magic blessing by the Fairies at the end of the play, all exploit this unusual verse-form and there is a fascinating variation on *this* in the final moments of III.ii, where Puck reduces the number of syllables to such simplicity that some lines contain only one metrical foot

On the ground

Sleep sound

I'll apply

To your eye,

Gentle lover, remedy

A favourite device of Shakespeare's is to provide a 'punch' to exit lines by using rhyming couplets. There are particularly effective examples of this technique in *A Midsummer Night's Dream* and any performer will vouch for the power that these give to an exit. Look, for instance, at the exits of Titania in II.i.144-5; Helena at lines 243-4 and Puck at lines 268-9. There are many other examples of which perhaps the double rhyme on the exits of Helena and Hermia in III.ii is the best (see lines 349, 350 and 351).

I suggested at the opening of the section on language that the language of a play both establishes the nature of the action and of the characters. We can see that movement from one verse form to another or a transition from verse to prose always achieves a change in atmosphere and pace. The contrasts may enhance the humour or tension of a scene and the patterns of language Shakespeare employs always have significance in the situation. For example, when Oberon and Titania are reconciled they dance a very formal and stately movement-pattern. This is reflected in the words spoken – which may, in fact, have been spoken over music – all eight lines rhyme in emphasis of perfect concord (see IV.i.83-90). In complete contrast there *is* a discernible pattern in the dialogue of Demetrius and Helena (II.i.188 onwards) with many repeated words but the effect is of discord because of the irregularity and antiphonal (the speaking of alternate voices) nature of the repetition. There are further examples of both devices in this play.

The language people speak reveals a great deal of their character and Shakespeare assigns quite different styles and forms to each of his groups of characters. Theseus and Hippolyta always speak in rather formal blank verse apart from their remarks during the performance of *Pyramus and Thisbe*, which are in prose. The 'Mechanicals' always speak *prose* – Shakespeare frequently used this technique to differentiate low-born characters – except when they use the highly contrived verse of their 'interlude'. The lovers speak blank verse and rhymed verse but their rhymes often seem shallow and over-elaborate whereas the Fairies, who also speak both blank and rhymed verse, have a language rich in vibrant imagery and full of mood and movement.

4.4 IMAGERY AND MYTHOLOGY

Imagery
When a playwright uses a word or visual effect to suggest *more* than the mere literal or commonplace meaning he is creating an 'image'. Imagery provides rich dimensions of meaning and can suggest related themes and new ideas; a single image can evoke many kinds of associations and provide a satisfying artistic experience for the audience by its appeal to the mind. An image is really the representation of an idea: what is seen and heard on stage has deeper implications. On the surface *A Midsummer Night's Dream* is a rather trite story but by clever use of imagery Shakespeare gives it profound significance and stimulates our imaginations.

The moon is mentioned more than thirty times in this play and there are several references to Diana (or Phoebe), goddess of the moon and chastity. In Shakespeare's time the moon was also thought to be the cause of dew so that Lysander speaks of moonlight as the time when

>   Phoebe doth behold
> Her silver visage in the watery glass,
> Decking with liquid pearl the bladed grass   (I.i.209-11)

and Titania says that the moon

>   looks with a wat'ry eye;
> And when she weeps, weeps every little flower   (III.ii.202-3)

In the Elizabethan theatre, devoid of any kind of artificial stage lighting, it would have been necessary to reinforce the fact that much of the action of the play was taking place by moonlight and Shakespeare relies on his language to achieve this. Just as *he* is determined to set his play in moonlight so *also* is Quince and we see the absurdity of trying to achieve the effect by visual means – neither the attempt to bring 'real' moonlight onto the stage nor a personification of Moonshine is nearly so successful as Shakespeare's method.

The moon governs not only tides and floods (see II.i.103) but the time-scale of the play. Theseus and Hippolyta are to be married at a time determined by the phase of the moon; Lysander has secretly wooed Hermia by moonlight; Hermia will escape 'with the moon's sphere'; Quince and his colleagues agree to meet by moonlight; Oberon and Titania are 'ill met by moonlight'; Pyramus and Thisbe meet by moonlight and the moon indicates to Titania that the time has come to lead Bottom to her bower.

The characters who are controlled by the moon's measure of time are also affected by its power. Diana, goddess of chastity, imposes her discipline on lustful humanity: Theseus and Hippolyta must wait to consummate their impatient desires in marriage until Diana allows, and Hermia's punishment for following *her* desires rather than her father's wishes will be, according to Theseus

> To live a barren sister all your life,
> Chanting faint hymns to the cold fruitless moon.   (I.i.72-3)

When the moon drops dew upon the flowers it is as if they are weeping for enforced loss of their chastity (III.ii.204), and even Flute knows that a paramour, the exact opposite of a chaste virgin, is 'a thing of naught'. To some extent, therefore, the play may be seen to pay homage to the ideal of virginity for which Queen Elizabeth 'the virgin goddess', was supposed to stand.

Yet the moon is also an agent of change. By its light things are made to look very different; as Theseus reminds us, 'How easy is a bush supposed a bear?' The shadows which move in the woods are created by the moon and the imaginings they prompt are often as insubstantial as the illusions of love which are prompted by faulty perception. That is why the lover is like the *lunatic* (someone traditionally affected by 'la lune' - the moon) and why Shakespeare's play exploits the traditional idea of Midsummer madness associated with the moon and applies it to lovers. Once they are in the moonlight the lovers are seized with insanity; reaons and logic are replaced by wild emotions governed by the deceived senses: even Bottom as Pyramus is affected, and in his direct address to the moon thanks it for its 'sunny beams' and its 'golden, glittering gleams' (V.i.287).

Diana, the virgin goddess, has another image: she is a huntress. Hippolyta likens the moon to a 'silver bow', the weapon of the huntress, in the opening scene and in the final scene of the play Puck refers to Diana, one of 'triple Hecate's team' who sweep through the world driving away darkness. Shakespeare involves Hippolyta herself in this imagery. She was an Amazon queen, traditionally a virgin warrior, and she also is a huntress. It is the hunt which finally wakes the lovers from their deluded sleep and, in the same way, the darkness of erotic love into which the young people have fallen is ended by the coming of light.

In exact opposition to Diana is Cupid, god of love, who works on the senses and arouses passion. Cupid's arrow, aimed at the virgin queen, missed its aim and fell on 'a little western flower' (II.i.66) and flowers are used throughout the play as images of sensuousness. Egeus complains that Lysander has seduced Hermia by giving her 'nosegays', and Hermia's cheeks are likened to fading roses when trouble overwhelms her love. Titania, with 'cowslips tall' as her attendants, luxuriates in a scented bed of wild thyme, oxlips, violets, woodbine, musk roses and eglantine and sends her Fairies to 'kill cankers in the musk-rose buds' (II.ii.3). When her passion for Bottom is reaching its climax, the Fairy Queen promises that he will sleep on 'pressed flowers', and also leads him to a 'flowery bed' and wants to 'stick musk-roses' in his 'sleek smooth head'. Finally, as she winds him in her arms she whispers that her embrace will be like 'honeysuckle' or 'ivy' (IV.i.40). When Oberon sees Titania with Bottom she has placed a garland of flowers around his temples, but Oberon notices that Diana's dew is on the flowers as if they are weeping at the absurd power of eroticism (IV.i.50).

The triumph of Diana over Cupid is given an image in the flowers because, finally, Oberon uses the juice from 'Dian's bud' to neutralise the effect of 'Cupid's flower' (see IV.i.71-2). In the same way that Shakespeare has created certain illusions and associations in the minds of his audience by his frequent references to the moon so, also, he evokes scents and colours by the mention of flowers. He parodies his own play by having the 'Mechanicals' introduce Moonshine and similarly makes an absurd comment on his use of the flowers and plants by having Thisbe speak these ridiculous lines over the body of Pyramus

> These lily lips,
> This cherry nose,
> These yellow cowslip cheeks,
> Are gone, are gone,
> Lovers, make moan –
> His eyes were green as leeks.   (V.i.322–8)

The ludicrous inappropriateness of these words can be very funny in performance and the interest is heightened by the fact that the *eyes* have consistently been employed as a symbol of physical attraction. Helena tells us that Lysander dotes on 'Hermia's eyes' (I.i.230) and dwells again on the power of Hermia's eyes (in II.ii.96 onwards) but the elaborate imagery with which Demetrius declares his love for Helena is, in its way, as clumsy and artificial as Thisbe's

> O Helen, goddess, nymph, perfect divine!
> To what, my love, shall I compare thine eyne?
> Crystal is muddy! O, how ripe in show
> Thy lips – those kissing cherries – tempting grow!   (III.ii.137–40)

Early in the play (I.i.183) Helena has likened Hermia's eyes to 'lodestars' and this image of the eyes as stars which guide travellers remains behind all the subsequent references to the power of the eyes. Just as moonlight provokes delusions there are also dangers in what Puck calls 'spangled starlight sheen'! (II.i.29).

Mythology
By setting his play in ancient Athens, the playwright evokes the sense of order that we associate with the architecture and law of classical civilisation – a sense which is lost once the action moves into the woods, where the trees and shadows contrast sharply with the columns and light of the city. Shakespeare is also able to exploit the sense of heroic deeds and close relationship between gods and men typified by Greek mythology. Theseus himself is a figure from mythology and his deeds included the defeat of the legendary Amazons together with the capture of their queen, Hippolyta; but some of his other achievements and adventures are mentioned by Oberon

> Didst though not lead him through the glimmering night
> From Perigenia, whom he ravished,
> And make him with fair Aegles break his faith,
> With Ariadne, and Antiopa? (II.i.77–80)

It is somewhat strange to equate the wordy and worthy Duke of Athens with the adventurer of such exploits and it is in some ways equally strange to hear Hippolyta, about to settle to an aristocratic life in something very much akin to rural England, talking about her experiences with Hercules - especially as he is one of the characters whom Bottom claims to be fond of acting.

The effect is to set the play out of time but to make sense of the rival claims on mortals of Diana, the moon goddess, and Cupid and to make the personification of the dawn as Aurora seem quite natural (see III.ii.387). Shakespeare uses both Ovid and Plutarch to provide starting points for his ideas, as in the legend of Cupid's 'love shaft' falling on the flower, but what he derives most from mythology is the sense of the gods' involvement in human affairs and in nature. The parallel in the play is the way in which the mortal Theseus and Hippolyta are both the subject of concern for the immortal Titania and Oberon who, in turn, have affected the lives of men by producing foul weather as a result of their quarrel.

A study of the play will reveal many references to mythological figures and ideas - these are listed below. (This does not include *Pyramus and Thisbe* or the entertainments offered to Theseus at his wedding.)

Diana (implied)	I.i.73, 209; II.i.156-63; III.ii.203
Diana	I.i.89; IV.i.71
Cupid	I.i.169, 235; II.i.157-65; III.ii.450; IV.i.71
Venus	I.i.171
Dido, Queen of Carthage	I.i.173
Aeneas	I.i.174
Hercules (Ercles)	I.ii.29, 40; IV.i.110; V.i.46
Phoebus (Phibbus)	I.ii.35
Fates	I.ii.38
Antiopa	II.i.80
Ariadne	II.i.80
Aegles	II.i.79
Perigenia	II.i.78
Hiems	II.i.109
Neptune	II.i.126; III.ii.399
Apollo	II.i.231
Daphne	II.i.231
Philomel	II.ii.13
Acheron	III.ii.364
Aurora	III.ii.387, 396
Hecate	V.i.376

If we add to these the fact that Quince is presenting a play based on mythology during which he draws on a wider range of classical reference we can see that Shakespeare laces his drama with the images, characters and stories of ancient Greece. These, however, are absorbed into a very English play with its folklore and anachronistic mention of St Valentine so that, although we can believe in Shakespeare's Athens, with its sharp law and its characters supposedly wearing Athenian garments, we also find something recognisable and familiar about the setting. This would have been more true for some members of an Elizabethan audience whose education was far more likely to have familiarised them with classical learning and yet whose contemporary world Shakespeare recreates in some measure in the play.

4.5 MUSIC AND DANCE

Many people imagine that the addition of music and dancing to the production of a play is an unnecessary frill to add a little extra excitement. Regrettably this is sometimes the case, but in Shakespeare's *A Midsummer Night's Dream* both music and dance are as much a part of the play as the words themselves. Shakespeare is quite specific about their inclusion and any interpretation which ignores them is greatly impoverished.

The earliest texts of this play in existence indicate the use of music and dancing at certain points but our general knowledge of Shakespeare might well lead us to believe that music, at least, was so widely used in his theatre that it may have occurred throughout a production of *A Midsummer Night's Dream*. It is certainly the case that many directors have felt the need to include a great deal of music as both an accompaniment to the songs and as a device for creating mood and atmosphere.

In one sense music is an extended metaphor for the action of this particular play because it is comprised both of discord and its resolution in harmony. Hippolyta refers to this feature in her appreciation of the Spartan hounds (IV.i.110-16) when she speaks of 'so musical a discord' and Theseus, who has claimed that his hounds produce a similarly pleasing effect, picks up the same theme when he greets the waking lovers with the question

>How comes this gentle concord in the world?   (IV.i.141)

This incident occurs just after Oberon and Titania have celebrated the new-found harmony of their marriage in a dance to music and the same couple show their blessings on the marriages of three other couples in the same way at the end of the play. It is significant, however, that the idea of the coexistence of discord and concord is never far from the surface in this play and is reflected in the description of *Pyramus and Thisbe* as 'very tragical mirth' and 'tedious and brief' and in the contradictions between the clarity and befuddlement with which Bottom, Titania and the lovers recall their dreams. Throughout the play, in fact, characters and relationships move from discord to harmony.

Music is often used in *A Midsummer Night's Dream* as a delightful relaxing diversion. Titania falls asleep to music (II.ii.9 onwards) and offers the same pleasure to Bottom (IV.i.26); Theseus looks to music as one of the pleasures that will fill the time (V.i.39), and Oberon and Titania call upon music to induce even deeper sleep in the troubled mortals who have become so confused in the woods. Ironically, both Titania and the lovers are also wakened at one point by particularly loud music: Titania by Bottom's singing and the lovers by the huntsmen's horns, and there is a good deal of humour in the contrast between the 'sweet music' which Titania obviously normally enjoys and Bottom's taste for the crude 'tongs and bones' (IV.i.28).

Perhaps more than anything else, music enhances the magic quality of *A Midsummer Night's Dream*. 'Magic songs' which influence the feelings of the characters were a familiar feature in Elizabethan poetry and drama and were usually sung by boy singers. We know that at one stage Shakespeare's company included a boy who was an able lutenist and we may assume that he would have sung 'You spotted snakes'. Unfortunately *A Midsummer Night's Dream* is one of the plays for which we do not have the original musical settings but as it was written at a time when England led the Western world in the quality of its lute songs the richness of the music can be imagined.

The obvious example of a 'magic song' is the lullaby which the Fairies sing to Titania shortly after the opening of II.ii. and there are many beautiful muscial settings to these words. The song does indeed create a sense of magic, it is like a charm which can only be broken by the even more powerful charm of Oberon. Its words are soft and the singers invite Philomel, the Nightingale, to sing with them. Because the rhythm is relaxed and there is the extended repetition of 'lulla, lullaby' the effect is to create an atmosphere of peace and tranquillity – an effect which can only be produced so well by music, and it is an invitation to dream.

Dance also has associations with harmony and magic; the 'roundel' which is performed in II.ii with the dancers joining hands in a circle, is both a symbol of unity and a 'fairy ring'. Titania challenges Oberon to 'patiently dance in our round' (II.i.140) or avoid her altogether and it is only when their relationship is restored that they dance (IV.i). The fact that a dance with music occurs at this point in the play has led many scholars to conjecture that this would have been an elaborate and stately dance very similar to those performed in court entertainments. It is, in fact, possible to prolong this part of the play to become a spectacular interlude, and in Jacobean times it became quite common for a small masque to be inserted into a play just before the final resolution of the action.

A very different form of dance is specified at the conclusion of *Pyramus and Thisbe*. The Bergomask was a crude, peasant dance, no doubt accompanied by the rather vulgar sounds of tongs, bones and other more primitive instruments. It was as heavy and earthbound as the roundel was light and airy but both dances had one thing in common: they both impose a sense of order on the performers. Once an individual starts to dance *with* others in a formation there is a discipline and form to what they are doing and in every case in *A Midsummer Night's Dream* a dance signifies a return to unity and order.

The need for the fairy characters to create a feeling of lightness and delicacy of movement has frequently led directors to cast trained dancers and often child dancers in these roles. Costume designs sometimes resemble designs for ballet and balletic movement is used to convey weightlessness. In the recent National Theatre production Titania played the entire performance on tiptoe and the Fairies dropped to the stage from a network of ropes - all in an attempt to appear 'of the air'. The dance-like quality of the play has, in fact, attracted many choreographers and Marius Petipa (1872), Michel Fokine (1902), George Balanchine (1962), Frederick Ashton (1964), Heinz Spoerli (1975) and Robert de Warren (1981) all created ballets from the play using Felix Mendelssohn's music, and a recent ballet by Tom Schilling with music by G. Katzer (1981) was entitled *A New Midsummer Night's Dream*.

It is a useful exercise for students to decide at which points in the stage play *they* would include music and dance. Stage directions tend to be unreliable - one early example calls for a fanfare of trumpets at the opening of *Pyramus and Thisbe* - but we do know that by the early years of this century the play was almost overwhelmed with incidental music. A producer at the Old Vic who attempted to remedy this by introducing simple folk airs was severely criticised by one member of the audience who said that she expected extra value from *A Midsummer Night's Dream* because it was both a play and an opera! This extraordinary view was almost entirely due to the sumptuous and brilliant music composed for the play by Mendelssohn in the early nineteenth century which became a standard requirement for many years. The famous Wedding March from the score is still used by many couples at their weddings, probably completely unaware of the piece's origin, but while Mendelssohn's music perfectly creates the play's atmosphere of magic and rustic humour it is felt by many modern directors to be unwieldy, obtrusive and 'dated'. Many composers have written alternative settings. Carl Orff, for example, has produced no fewer than six, yet Shakespeare almost certainly used the music that was best for the particular conditions in which the play was performed, sometimes using existing material and sometimes having new material composed. This is probably the best model to follow.

4.6 *A MIDSUMMER NIGHT'S DREAM* IN THE THEATRE

In our analysis of the play so far we have seen that *A Midsummer Night's Dream* contains may psychological insights, much wonderful poetry and some memorable characters. Above all, however, we are dealing with a work of superb theatrical craftsmanship. Shakespeare wrote the play to exploit the features of a bare, open stage with two entrance doors on either side at the rear and possibly some form of inner stage. Such features could have been found in an Elizabethan theatre but also in a great hall, in which the first performance of *A Midsummer Night's Dream* might have taken place. Scenery and scene changes of the sort to which we may have become accustomed were unnecessary. Notice how Shakespeare first establishes the context and sometimes the location of each scene in the opening lines of the scenes

THESEUS	Now, fair Hippolyta, our nuptial hour Draws on apace (I.ii)
QUINCE	Is all our company here? (I.ii)
PUCK	How now, spirit, whither wander you? (II.i)
BOTTOM	Are we all met?
QUINCE	Pat, pat; and here's a marvellous convenient place for our rehearsal. This green plot shall be our stage, this hawthorn brake our tiring-house. . . (III.i)

and how he paints the scenery in the minds of the audience

FAIRY	Over hill, over dale, Thorough bush, thorough brier, Over park, over pale, Thorough flood, thorough fire (II.i)
PUCK	And now they never meet in grove or green By fountain clear, or spangled starlight sheen, (II.i)
LYSANDER	Fair love, you faint with wand'ring in the wood; And – to speak truth – I have forgot our way. . .

HERMIA   Be it so, Lysander; find you out a bed,
            For I upon this bank will rest my head   (II.ii)

No doubt you will be able to recall many similar examples; Oberon's description of Titania's bower, also upon a bank, Puck's and Oberon's descriptions of sunrise, numerous references to the colours, sounds and scents of nature and the many evocations of darkness and moonlight. By such descriptions Shakespeare also makes any form of artifical lighting redundant, and it is significant that the two suggestions for the introduction of moonlight into *Pyramus and Thisbe* are both equally ridiculous (see III.ii.45-59). Through the discoveries of the 'Mechanicals' the playwright does, however, suggest that certain *symbolic* items of scenery (the wall, for example) are very effective on the bare stage and it is likely that the occasional tree, throne or bank would have been used in performance.

The twin entrances from the rear onto a broad open stage made for powerful appearances and fluid movement. As one set of characters left the stage through one door another set would already have appeared from the other. Examples of this are to be found in the transitions from II.ii to III.i, the exit of the Fairies and the entrance of the court in IV.i.100 and the entrance of Puck in V.i.363. Particularly effective use of the appearance of characters at *both* doors is made at the opening of Act II and, of course, at the meeting of Oberon and Titania later in the same Act (line 60).

A character entering at one of these doors would generally be seen by the audience before meeting the other characters and that distance which an entering character would have to travel before reaching the main acting area would often give a chance for them to be introduced

LYSANDER   Keep promise, love. Look, her comes Helena.   (I.i.179)
PUCK   But room, Fairy! Here Comes Oberon.
FAIRY   And here my mistress.   (II.i.58-9)

Think also of the comic, startling effect of Bottom's two great entrances from *behind* the other characters and of the way in which the lovers, rushing in and out, would have used those two doors.

The flow of the action of the play is also enhanced by the fact that Shakespeare quite often leaves characters from one scene either asleep on stage or watching while a further scene is played out and we can speculate that what we have described as a 'discovery space' (see page 81) might have been used for Titania's bower to enable vigorous action to continue all over the rest of the stage.

We are, in fact, provided with a clue as to the way in which the 'tiring house' (see page 81) was used as the place where the actors waited for their next entrance. This comes in Act III when Quince, having described a hawthorn bush as their tiring house, says

> When you have spoken your speech, enter into that brake;
> and so every one according to his cue. (72-4)

Other insights into the workings of the Elizabethan theatre are also provided by Quince and his men in the course of their rehearsals: Quince would have been the only member of the company with the 'book of the play'; he was the 'teller' who directed rehearsals. The other actors had a scroll with their own parts plus the last words (the 'cues') of the previous speaker written down. This is the part which Snug was asking for (I.ii.67) and it accounts for the mistake made by Flute at the rehearsal (III.i.95-7) in speaking all his lines and the cues at once. Snug's anxiety to have his part was because of his being 'slow of study', and this was a great drawback for actors as it meant 'slow at learning lines'. The 'quick study' actor was an asset to any company in those days, as they changed the plays they were performing with great frequency.

We learn a little about Elizabethan acting too: it was obviously common for them to wear false beards (see I.ii.89) and soft shoes (IV.ii.34-5). Some, certainly, could expect court favour (IV.ii.21-2) and in this play, as in *Hamlet*, Shakespeare appears to be holding up for ridicule an inflated and highly artificial acting style - this was particularly the case with the part of the 'tyrant', the ranting, strutting role such as that of Herod in the medieval mystery plays with which we know Shakespeare was familiar. Almost every generation of actors likes to scoff at what they consider to be the 'old school' of acting and Shakespeare was no exception; he was also keenly aware that outmoded styles of performance are frequently preserved by amateurs long after they have disappeared from the professional stage.

Shakespeare was equally critical of some of the plays of his age and much of the material he gives to the 'Mechanicals' is a wicked parody of popular drama: the title of their play, *The Most Lamentable Comedy and Most Cruel Death of Pyramus and Thisbe* is a mockery of the titles and authors' descriptions of plays from the 1560s and 70s, particularly, perhaps, Preston's *Cambises*, a popular early play from the period, and we must note that Quince refers to their play as an 'interlude', which was the common Elizabethan term for a short dramatic piece. The appalling verse which Bottom speaks impromptu to show his powers as a 'tyrant' is very much like some passages in John Hudley's translation of *Hercules Oetaeus* by Seneca (1581), but even worse is to come. Both in the rehearsal and performance of *Pyramus and Thisbe* we have language which is perversely archaic, ludicrously inappropriate, full of extravagant images and poetic devices - all of which point to Shakespeare's awareness of the potential falseness of the plays still being performed in his day. We can say also with some certainty that Bottom's speech to the wall

> And thou, O wall, O sweet, O lovely wall... (V.i.173)

is a parody of Golding's translation of Ovid's *Metamorphoses* from which Shakespeare took the story of Pyramus and Thisbe.

Shakespeare does have something to say about modes of presentation and audiences. In the 'play within a play' both in *A Midsummer Night's Dream* and *Hamlet* the players perform a 'prologue' showing in mime or 'dumb show' the outline of the plot, and the subsequent action continues to use much direct address to the audience. The audience, on the other hand, feel free to comment noisily on the action and even sit on the stage itself. It was not until the time of the great actor David Garrick (1717-79) that the audience in the English theatre was finally excluded from sitting on the stage itself and until that time it was quite common for discussions and unfriendly exchanges to take place between members of the audience and the cast. If you, like me, become irritated by the constant 'witty' remarks of the lovers during the performance of *Pyramus and Thisbe* then you may feel that Shakespeare was trying to educate his audience to greater sensitivity. It is particularly interesting that at the 1983-84 production of *A Midsummer Night's Dream* by the National Theatre the audience were invited to sit on cushions on the stage.

A Midsummer Night's Dream has been subjected to many interpretations and adaptations. Within fifty years of the playwright's death a comic interlude entitled *Bottom the Weaver* had been created for separate performance and the English composer Purcell soon used Shakespeare's original play as the basis for his opera *The Fairy Queen*. Various corrupted versions of the play continued to be popular and it was not until 1839 that the actor-manager Charles Mathews restored the original text in performance. Nineteenth-century productions had to cater for the prudish attitudes of the audience and the growing taste for spectacular presentations which developed with various advances in theatre technology. Consequently there was a tendency to concentrate on the magical, fairy qualities of the play.

One of the most famous of such productions was that by Ludwig Tieck in Berlin (1842) for which Mendelssohn wrote the incidental music and another by the English actor-manager Samuel Phelps (1804-78) was played largely behind a scrim (an open fabric used in upholstery) which produced a misty effect. Realistic and lush settings for *A Midsummer Night's Dream* reached their ultimate in 1900 when Herbert Beerbohm Tree mounted a production in London which included live rabbits scampering over a carpet of grass from which real flowers grew. The complex changes of scenery added forty-five minutes to the running time of the play but its popularity was immense – the production being visited by 220,000 people.

Twentieth-century productions have often tried to break away from the prettiness of those earlier interpretations in an attempt to rediscover Shakespeare's original intentions. Although it is rarely possible to disregard all the advances of stage lighting and scenic construction, there has been a move towards types of open staging that more nearly resemble the stages of Shakespeare's day than the picture-frame 'proscenium arch' theatres built on Nineteenth-century lines. Efforts have also been made to re-examine the themes of the play with the result that far more than a comic fairy story has emerged.

The interpretation of the Fairies always poses a major problem for the director because they have to be made credible to a contemporary audience. Harley Granville-Barker's famous production of 1913–14 solved the problem of the Fairies by having them all dressed in gold, thereby giving them a strangeness which avoided the 'prettiness' of many productions.

In one Royal Shakespeare Company production all the Fairies except Oberon, Titania and Puck were puppets with disembodied voices, in another they were naked satyrs. Oberon and Titania have been presented as wearing rich Elizabethan costumes, whereas they were simply dressed in leaves in a recent film. A television version had the King and Queen of Fairies meeting on horseback and Puck as a cockney who spoke his verse as if it were doggerel.

Perhaps the most famouse of all modern productions was that by Peter Brook in 1970. Brook portrayed the Fairies as menacing beings who entangled all mortals entering their domain in a terrible web; but this was only one of the unusual features of the production. The setting was a white box with twin doors at the rear and with catwalks above from which actors not participating in a scene watched the action. From time to time trapezes were let down and an acrobatic cast, dressed mainly like circus performers, swung and balanced their way through the play, sometimes becoming entangled in coils of wire which were the nearest the setting ever came to representing trees. Bottom, in cloth cap and string vest, and all the other 'Mechanicals' were played with great seriousness and there was a strong emphasis on crude sexuality.

For many critics and members of the audience Brook's production was a revelation – a liberation from years of cloying romanticism; for others, it was an outrage that distorted Shakespeare's text and intentions. Books have been devoted to descriptions and analyses of this particular production but this remarkable play continues to attract and excite new interpretations. There have been several film versions and in 1967 the choreographer George Balanchine created a film from his ballet of *A Midsummer Night's Dream*. More recently still the composer Benjamin Britten wrote an opera of the same name which had a notable production by Peter Hall in which the woodland setting was created by actors dressed as trees.

It is essential in your study that you give detailed consideration as to how *you* would stage the play. The possibilities seem endless but the decisions must be based on a thorough understanding of Shakespeare's text and of the performance demands embedded in it.

5 SPECIMEN PASSAGE AND COMMENTARY

The following example shows the kind of close critical attention that is necessary for an analysis of part of the text. You cannot really claim to 'know' the play unless you have approached the entire text with this sort of care and to enable you to do this effectively I am suggesting a number of important stages in such an analysis.

First we must establish the *context* of the passage, understanding clearly the events that have given rise to the action covered by the extract being studied: in any examination answer, however, this must be stated *briefly*. Secondly, there must be an appreciation of *what is going on* both in terms stage action and the psychological state of the various characters. Then we must turn specifically to the *language*, examining its style, content and the way in which it creates the dramatic effect such as atmosphere, tension, irony or climax. Initially we may need to ensure a complete understanding of obscure words or sentence structure and to be particularly wary of words that have changed their meaning since Shakespeare's day. For a proper appreciation of the content of a passage it may also be necessary to familiarise oneself with beliefs, attitudes and tastes of Elizabethan times, or with some contemporary event, and a good scholarly edition of the play should be particularly helpful in this respect. In the case of *A Midsummer Night's Dream*, for example, some familiarity with Elizabethan courtly love poetry – especially some sixteenth-century sonnets – will shed light on the expression of an idealised view of feminine beauty which Shakespeare parodies in this play. Above all we must remember this is a *play* we are considering, designed for performance in a theatre.

5.1 SPECIMEN PASSAGE

Act II, Scene ii, lines 72–113

Enter PUCK

PUCK: Through the forest have I gone,
But Athenian found I none
On whose eyes I might approve
This flower's force in stirring love.
Night and silence – Who is here?
Weeds of Athens he doth wear.
This is he, my master said
Despisèd the Athenian maid;
And here the maiden, sleeping sound
On the dank and dirty ground.
Pretty soul! she durst not lie
Near this lack-love, this kill-courtesy.
Churl, upon thy eyes I throw
All the power this charm doth owe.
When thou wak'st, let love forbid
Sleep his seat on thy eyelid.

He squeezes the flower juice on LYSANDER's eyelids

So, awake when I am gone;
For I must now to Oberon. *Exit*

Enter DEMETRIUS and HELENA, running

HELENA: Stay, though thou kill me, sweet Demetrius!
DEMETRIUS: I charge thee hence; and do not haunt me thus.
HELENA: O, wilt thou darkling leave me? Do not so.
DEMETRIUS: Stay, on thy peril: I alone will go. *Exit*
HELENA: O, I am out of breath in this fond chase!
The more my prayer, the lesser is my grace.
Happy is Hermia, whereso'er she lies,
For she hath blessèd and attractive eyes.
How came her eyes so bright? Not with salt tears –
If so, my eyes are oft'ner washed than hers.
No, no, I am as ugly as a bear,
For beasts that meet me run away for fear.
Therefore no marvel though Demetrius
Do as a monster fly my presence thus.
What wicked and dissembling glass of mine
Made me compare with Hermia's sphery eyne?
But who is here? Lysander! on the ground!

> Dead? or asleep? I see no blood, no wound.
> Lysander, if you live, good sir, awake!
>
> LYSANDER: (*Awaking*) And run through fire I will for
> thy sweet sake.
> Transparent Helena, Nature shows art,
> That through thy bosom makes me see thy heart.
> Where is Demetrius? O, how fit a word
> Is that vile name to perish on my sword!

5.2 COMMENTARY

Oberon has watched Demetrius rejecting Helena's love after she has followed him into the wood and has sent Puck to squeeze love juice into Demetrius's eye to remedy the situation. Puck, however, comes across Hermia and Lysander sleeping some distance apart and thinking that this and the fact that they are wearing Athenian clothes ('weeds of Athens') confirms they are the quarrelling lovers he is seeking, squeezes juice into Lysander's eyes. Puck leaves before realising his mistake but *the audience* is immediately reminded of it by the running entrance of Demetrius with Helena in pursuit. Helena is left behind, out of breath, and in a soliloquy despairs of her chances, reckoning herself unattractive and envying Hermia who is loved by both men. She does not notice Hermia but she does notice and wake the sleeping Lysander who, under the influence of the love juice, declares his love for her.

Puck enters carrying an agent of magic and his rhyming couplets of seven syllables (seven being a magic number) create a sense of the charm he is holding. His opening lines remind the audience both of Athens and that the current action is in a forest. The movement is light and nimble as befits Puck, the rhythmic structure the same as when Oberon put the spell on Titania's eyes. The potency of the magic juice is evoked in the line 'This flower's force in stirring love' and Puck seeks eyes on which to test ('approve') its power. There is a moment of stillness in which Shakespeare reminds his audience of the fact that the action takes place in the darkness of night before Puck sees Lysander. A slightly longer line concludes the section of the speech in which Puck convinces himself that he has found Helena and Demetrius. His attitude to them is already established by Oberon – his *sympathy* for the woman, described as a 'Pretty soul' established by the alliteration of 'sleeping sound' and 'dank and dirty' – yet alliteration also gives *emphasis* to his distaste for the man who is dismissed as a 'lack-love' and 'kill-courtesy'. Ironically, this is precisely what Lysander is *about* to become as a result of Puck's error.

Puck squeezes the juice with an incantation-like spell, wishing that love will so obsess the recipient that he will be unable to sleep.

The sudden entrance of Demetrius and Helena highlights Puck's mistake immediately and introduces another of the abrupt changes of tempo with which the play abounds: sleeping, waking, running and stopping with exhaustion alternate and build the sense of confusion and bewilderment. The iambic couplets of the lovers contrast with Puck's seven-syllable couplets. Helena's first words pick up the theme of her last exit (II.i.244) when she expressed her determination to die at Demetrius's hand. Her desire to die rather than lose her love illustrates the extremity of her predicament but the rhyming lines which the two young people call at each other alternately (stichomythia) have an artificial effect which, coupled with the fact that 'slaying for love' was a common courtly poetic metaphor, prevents the audience taking the scene too seriously, and indeed creates a comic effect. When Helena implores Demetrius not to leave her 'darkling' she not only means in the physical darkness of the night but the darkness of misery.

The misery of the jilted lover is captured in Helena's soliloquy – here the flow of the decasyllabic lines is slower and the rhyming couplets enhance the sense of pattern so that the speech, though much nearer to natural speech than Lysander's words which follow it, still has a degree of formality and unreality. That unreality is reinforced by the intensity with which Helena convinces herself that she is utterly ugly even though her mirror has shown her to have eyes as attractive as Hermia's. The mirror, she argues, must be wicked and dishonest – no wonder then that Demetrius runs from her. She grossly exaggerates when she mentions that animals are frightened by her ugliness but this loss of confidence is to be expected after Demetrius's treatment of her. She betrays an awareness that her whole enterprise in following Demetrius was foolish by the words 'fond chase', and then concentrates on the attractiveness of Hermia's eyes which she has continually blamed (compare I.i.183 and 230) for her misfortune. This is ironic because her eyes will shortly be praised by Lysander (II.ii.127) and the eyes are shown to be the instruments of faulty perception. The idea that the eye or any other part of the body should be an object of obsessive and exaggerated praise was part of the rhetorical tradition of Elizabethan love poetry. Such idealisation of woman's beauty was removed from real experience and at this point in the play Helena is caught between a desire for romantic love and harsh reality.

The rhythm of her speech and the flood of her misery is interrupted by her noticing Lysander sleeping. The audience know what to expect when she wakes him but she does not, and this adds tension to the moment. Even so, the audience experience some tense anticipation as they wait to see if the love juice has 'worked'.

It is as if Lysander has already been declaring his passionate love for years as he wakes with the words 'And run through fire I will for thy sweet sake' – like another line of a poem long since begun. Even in these first five lines his claims are more extravagant than anything uttered so far and their suddenness, surprise and high-flown poetic style must be overwhelming to Helena whose reaction can only be shock, incredulity and disbelief. There is an enormous contrast between Lysander's description of Helena and her own self-description. Lysander calls Helena 'transparent' – luminous and glorious, but then riddles cleverly like a courtier and suggests that nature has created her so exquisitely that through her bosom he can see her heart. Having fancied that he has access to the very seat of Helena's emotions Lysander turns heroic and declares he will impale his rival on his sword. Under the influence of the love juice Lysander has become irrational and absurd; his words in sharp contrast to the tender promise he made as he slept (II.ii.69).

In the course of this extract we see many of the play's major themes in action: magic, change, 'love at first sight', the agony of the jilted lover, reality and illusion are all essential ingredients.

6 CRITICAL APPRAISALS

Actors and directors tend, quite understandably, to regard critics with suspicion because they know that adverse criticism can seriously damage the success of a production and that sometimes theatre critics have a power out of all proportion to their actual knowledge of the theatre. Students, similarly, ought to be wary of the other kind of critic: the literary critic who publishes books and essays about plays; for we must always remember that simply because something is in print, it is not necessarily to be accepted without question. Both sorts of critic, however objective they try to be, reveal something of their own prejudices and reflect the beliefs and values of their day and subsequent scholarship may sometimes prove them wrong. However, the work of experienced critics who have given careful attention to a play or its production can be extremely valuable to students in providing fresh insights and opinions backed up by evidence from the text or from the conditions surrounding the play's composition.

The most impressive 'critical response' to *A Midsummer Night's Dream* is the continuing popularity of the play, for not only does it have more productions than any other Shakespeare play, it also has more performances than almost any play in the English Language. No wonder, therefore, that it has provoked so much wide and varied comment. Printed below is a small sample of such responses: firstly there are general comments concerning the nature of part or all of the play; and secondly, some critical responses to the play in performance. These short quotations from longer pieces are *not* intended for learning by heart, although some are indeed memorable; they are intended as a starting-point for your own thoughts and discussions; you are not expected to agree with them all or to accept the opinions expressed, but, remember, if you *disagree* you must back up your opinion with evidence from the play itself. You should particularly note the changes in style and content of the literary criticisms in different periods and the occasions when a production clearly achieved aspects of the playwright's intentions and when it obviously failed to do so!

6.1 GENERAL CRITICISMS OF THE PLAY

...and then to the King's Theatre, where we saw *Midsummer nights dreame*, which I had never seen before, nor shall ever again, for it is the most insipid ridiculous play that ever I saw in my life.

(Samuel Pepys 1662)

...poets may be allowed the...liberty for describing things which really exist not, if they are founded on popular belief. Of this nature are fairies ...and the extraordinary effects of magic; for 'tis still an imitation, though of other men's fancies; and thus [is] Shakespeare's.. *Midsummer Night's Dream* to be defended.

(John Dryden 1677)

I know not why Shakespear calls this play a *Midsummer Night's Dream*, when he so carefully informs us that is happened on the night preceding *May* day.

(Samuel Johnson 1765)

Wild and fantastical as this play is, all the parts in their various modes are well written and give the kind of pleasure which the author designed.

(Samuel Johnson 1773)

The...piece has great poetical and dramatic merit, considered in general; but a puerile plot, and odd mixture of incidents, and a forced connexion of various stiles, throw a kind of shade over that blaze of merit many passages would otherwise have possessed. There is no character strongly marked, yet the whole shews a very great master dallying with his own genius and imagination in a wonderful and delightful manner.

(Anon. 1774)

In the *Midsummer Night's Dream* alone, we should imagine, there is more sweetness and beauty of description than in the whole range of French poetry put together.

(William Hazlitt 1817)

The *Midsummer Night's Dream* is too exquisite a composition to be dulled by the infliction of philosophical analysis.

(J. Halliwell-Phillipps 1879)

A Midsummer Night's Dream is a psychological study, not of a solitary man, but of a spirit that unites mankind...The sentiment of such a play, so far as it can be summed up at all, can be summed up in one sentence, It is the mysticism of happiness.

(G. K. Chesterton 1904)

A Midsummer Night's Dream is more of a masque than a drama – an entertainment rather than a play. The characters are mostly puppets, and scarcely any except Bottom has the least psychological interest for the reader.

(Frank Sidgwick 1908)

[Note this writer's failure to understand that a play is to be performed and seen, nor simply read.]

So recklessly happy in writing such verse does Shakespeare grow that even the quarrel of the four lovers is stayed by a charming speech of Helena's thirty-seven lines long.

(Harley Granville-Barker 1914)

Here the quick ardours, the inconstancies, the caprices, the illusions, the delusions, every sort of love folly, become embodied and weave a world of their own. . .in such a way that everything is equally real or equally fantastic, as you may please to call it.

(Benetto Croce 1920)

In *A Midsummer Night's Dream* most – not all – of the dances are vitally connected with the plot. For instance, Titania's awakening in IVi is an important point in the play, for it is the point where the ravel begins to be untangled, and the occasion is celebrated by a dance of reunion.

(Enid Welsford 1927)

But of all our persons Theseus is the calmest and wisest. . .He shows an exquisite and wide love and deep human knowledge.

(G. Wilson Knight 1932)

In this play we are given three wholly distinct kinds of fairies.

(Ernest Schanzer 1955)

While the theme of love-madness weaves together various apparently unrelated portions of *A Midsummer Night's Dream* Shakespeare creates unity of atmosphere chiefly by flooding the play with moonlight. There is only one daylight scene in the entire play.

(Ernest Schanzer 1955)

Commensurate with its origins in a court marriage, this drama speaks throughout for a sophisticated Renaissance philosophy of the nature of love in both its rational and irrational forms.

(Paul Olson 1957)

I should myself be prepared to maintain that *A Midsummer Night's Dream* is Shakespeare's best comedy.

(Frank Kermode 1961)

For many years editors and critics have customarily praised *A Midsummer Night's Dream* for its artistic fusion of seemingly disparate elements.

Sometimes the praise involves little, really, beyond admiring the skill with which Shakespeare interwove the actions of the four lovers, the fairies, and the mechanicals in the first four acts of the play.

(R. W. Dent 1864)

The *Dream* is the most erotic of Shakespeare's plays.

(Jan Kott 1964)

Each set of characters plays its part under the auspices of the moon, the measure, in Theseus's and Hippolyta's opening speeches, of the interval of time which is the only remaining impediment to their union.

(Harold Brooks 1979)

The fairy king and queen are immediately established as powerful dramatic characters who have both human passions and more than human influence over the affections of other people.

(Roger Warren 1983)

In the case of the fairies Shakespeare is to be credited with the creation, single-handed, of an entirely new world. . .both benevolent and mysterious.

(G. K. Hunter 1962)

A Midsummer Night's Dream is the first of Shakespeare's plays that can be described without qualification, as a masterpiece. If he had written nothing else but this, his place would have been secure on the summit of Parnassus.

(Robert Speaight 1977)

The play has a strongly delineated moral theme or idea, namely, the irrationality of love, embodied most powerfully in its great central symbolic picture of the beautiful Queen of the fairies. . .wakening to dote on the monstrous Bottom.

(G. J. Watson 1983)

A brilliant play about magic.

(John Goodwin 1979)

6.2 THEATRE CRITICISMS

Quite masterly was the delivery by Mr. Phelps of the speech of Bottom on awakening. He was still a man subdued, but subdued by the sudden plunge into a state of unfathomable wonder. His dream clings about him, and still we are made to feel that his reality itself is but a fiction

(Henry Morley on Samuel Phelps's production 1853)

He allows the music to follow the play merely as a new fairy who sprinkles several tunes over the scene as a form of consecration prior to the entry of the spiritual procession, giving it wings upon which it can fly away. Only when the dialogue with all of its dramatis personae have receded into the background does the music hover over the forest as a sort of mist of recollection.

(Bjornson on Mendelssohn's music for the play used in a production of 1865)

Miss Lillian Swain in the part of Puck...announces her ability to girdle the earth in forty minutes in the attitude of a professional skater, and then begins the journey awkwardly in a swing, which takes her in the opposite direction to that in which she indicated her intention of going.

(George Bernard Shaw on a production of 1895)

Barker admitted that the fairies were the 'producer's test,' and that it was partly in the hope of passing that test that he had decided to produce the play at all. They could not sound too beautiful, but 'how should they look?'

(Robert Speaight on Granville-Barker's production of 1914)

Perhaps no feature of this 'show' awakened more discussion than Mr. Barker's fairies. From head to foot they were differentiated by a coat of bronze paint.

(George Odell on the same production)

However, when Guthrie revived the play in 1937 at Christmas time, with decor by Oliver Messel, and the fairies were straight out of an early Victorian ballet and of the Mendelssohn period, then the music was delightful, as indeed was the whole production. Helpmann as Oberon, looking like some strange, sinister stag beetle, was indeed a spirit of another sort.

(Harcourt Williams on an Old Vic production)

The Actors' Workshop production of *A Midsummer Night's Dream* was inspired – disastrously – by Jan Kott, for whom that particular dream is an erotic nightmare. The set and costumes were designed by the pop artist, Jim Dine...Hippolyta appeared in a cage, a light bulb flashed on and off in Demetrius's codpiece.

(Robert Speaight on a 1966 production in San Francisco)

Only a humourless man could have staged this.

(Benedict Nightingale on Peter Brook's 1970 production)

By creating a kind of clean, stark gymnasium...for the setting...the director and designer ignored many of the words of the text, especially the ambiguous, gentle and homely words in which the play abounds.

(John Russell Brown on the same production)

The performance passed from vaudeville knockabout deep into nightmare, and from simple truth to complex illusion. In its turn, the audience was

moved from fear to laughter, and from raptness in silence to open exhilaration. And the actors, beginning from diffidence and coldness, had in the end achieved a warm and intimate relation with the spectators.
(David Selbourne on the same production)

– magnificent in detail, but short in rustic enchantment.
(T. C. Kemp on the 1949 Stratford production)

Robin Phillips took as his starting-point Oberon's vision of the imperial votaress. . .he placed Elizabeth herself at the centre of the play, interpreting Titania and Hippolyta (played by the same actress), as aspects of the Queen's personality. The whole play became, as it were, a dream of Queen Elizabeth's.
(Roger Warren on the 1976 Stratford Ontario production)

His interpretation was rather low-key, serious, even sombre. When Lysander and Demetrius argued over Hermia, for instance, threat and counter-threat were spoken in hardly more than whispers, in obvious awe of a stern, inflexible Theseus.
(Roger Warren on the BBC TV production 1981)

REVISION QUESTIONS

These questions may be used for examination practice or as topics for revision

1. How does Shakespeare create an atmosphere of magic in this play?

2. To what extent is *A Midsummer Night's Dream* 'drenched in moonlight' and what dramatic purpose is served by the image of the moon?

3. How does this play explore the relationship between dreams and reality?

4. Show how *A Midsummer Night's Dream* deals with *one* of the following pairs of contrasts:
   (a) reality and imagination
   (b) reason and irrationality
   (c) concord and discord.

5. Why is music an integral part of the action of this play?

6. Examine the use which Shakespeare makes of dancing in *A Midsummer Night's Dream*.

7. What views of human love do we gain from this play?

8. To what extent does *A Midsummer Night's Dream* present love as a kind of madness?

9. How does *A Midsummer Night's Dream* celebrate both the event and idea of marriage?

10. Hermia, Titania, the four lovers and Bottom all awake from dreams. Comment on each of these moments both in the context of the action and of the thematic issues raised.

11. In what ways does *A Midsummer Night's Dream* examine the nature of drama itself?

12. Show how Shakespeare created this play for presentation on an Elizabethan stage.
13. Illustrate the nature and function of the varying verse forms in *A Midsummer Night's Dream*.
14. Discuss the distinctive role of Puck, Oberon or Theseus.
15. 'The shallowest thickskin of that barren sort' – comment on Puck's evaluation of Bottom.

APPENDIX: SHAKESPEARE'S THEATRE

We should speak, as Muriel Bradbrook remind us, not of the Elizabethan stage but of Elizabethan stages. Plays of Shakespeare were acted on tour, in the halls of mansions, one at least in Gray's Inn, frequently at Court, and after 1609 at the Blackfriars, a small, roofed theatre for those who could afford the price. But even after his Company acquired the Blackfriars, we know of no play of his not acted (unless, rather improbably, *Troilus* is an exception) for the general public at the Globe, or before 1599 at its predecessor, The Theatre, which, since the Globe was constructed from the same timbers must have resembled it. Describing the Globe, we can claim therefore to be describing, in an acceptable sense, Shakespeare's theatre, the physical structure his plays were designed to fit. Even in the few probably written for a first performance elsewhere, adaptability to that structure would be in his mind.

For the facilities of the Globe we have evidence from the drawing of the Swan theatre (based on a sketch made by a visitor to London about 1596) which depicts the interior of another public theatre; the builder's contract for the Fortune theatre, which in certain respects (fortunately including the dimensions and position of the stage) was to copy the Globe; indications in the dramatic texts; comments, like Ben Jonson's on the throne let down from above by machinery; and eye-witness testimony to the number of spectators (in round figures, 3000) accommodated in the auditorium.

In communicating with the audience, the actor was most favourably placed. Soliloquising at the centre of the front of the great platform, he was at the mid-point of the theatre, with no one among the spectators more than sixty feet away from him. That platform-stage (Figs I and II) was the most important feature for performance at the Globe. It had the audience - standing in the yard (10) and seated in the galleries (9) - on three sides of it. It was 43 feet wide, and 27½ feet from front to back. Raised (?5½ feet) above the level of the yard, it had a trap-door (II.8) giving access to the space below it. The actors, with their equipment, occupied the 'tiring house' (attiring-house: 2) immediately at the back of the stage. The stage-direction 'within' means inside the tiring-house. Along its frontage, probably from the top of the second storey, juts out the canopy or 'Heavens', carried on two large pillars rising through the platform (6, 7) and sheltering the rear part of the stage, the rest of which, like the yard, was open to the sky. If the 'hut' (I.8), housing the machinery for descents, stood, as in the Swan drawing, above the 'Heavens', that covering must have had a trap-door, so that the descents could be made through it.

Descents are one illustration of the vertical dimension the dramatist could use to supplement the playing-area of the great platform. The other opportunities are provided by the tiring-house frontage or facade. About this facade the evidence is not as complete or clear as we should like, so that Fig. I is in part conjectural. Two doors giving entry to the platform there certainly were (3). A third (4) is probable but not certain. When curtained, a door, most probably this one, would furnish what must be termed a discovery-space (II.5), not an inner stage (on which action in any depth would have been out of sight for a significant part of the audience). Usually no more than two actors were revealed (exceptionally, three), who often then moved out on to the platform. An example of this is Ferdinand and Miranda in *The Tempest* 'discovered' at chess, then seen on the platform speaking with their fathers. Similarly, the gallery (I.5) was not an upper stage. Its use was not limited to the actors; sometimes it functioned as 'lords' rooms' for favoured spectators, sometimes, perhaps, as a muscians' gallery. Frequently the whole gallery would not be needed for what took place aloft: a window-stage (as in the first balcony scene in *Romeo*, even perhaps in the second) would suffice. Most probably this would be a part (at one end) of the gallery itself; or just possibly, if the gallery did not (as it does in the Swan drawing) extend the whole width of the tiring-house, a window over the left- or right-hand door. As the texts show, whatever was presented aloft, or in the discovery-space, was directly related to the action on the platform, so that at no time was there left, between the audience and the action of the drama, a great bare space of platform-stage. In relating Shakespeare's drama to the physical conditions of the theatre, the primacy of that platform is never to be forgotten.

HAROLD BROOKS

Note: The present brief account owes most to C. Walter Hodges, *The Globe Restored*; Richard Hosley in *A New Companion to Shakespeare Studies*, and in *The Revels History of English Drama*; and to articles by Hosley and Richard Southern in *Shakespeare Survey*, 12, 1959, where full discussion can be found.

SHAKESPEARE'S THEATRE
The stage and its adjuncts; the tiring-house; and the auditorium.

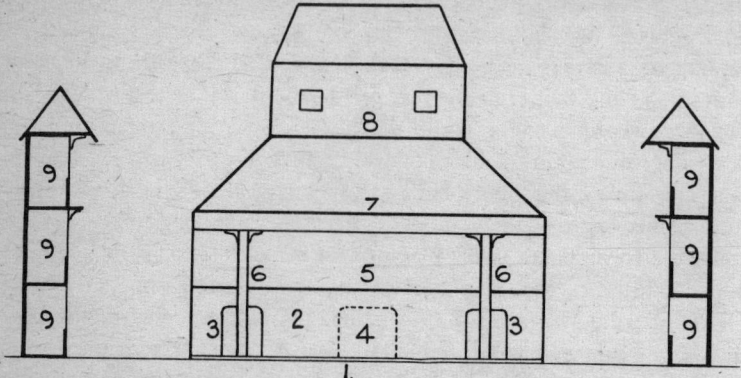

FIG I ELEVATION
1. Platform stage (approximately five feet above the ground) 2. Tiring-house 3. Tiring-house doors to stage 4. Conjectural third door 5. Tiring-house gallery (balustrade and partitioning not shown) 6. Pillars supporting the heavens 7. The heavens 8. The hut 9. The spectators' galleries

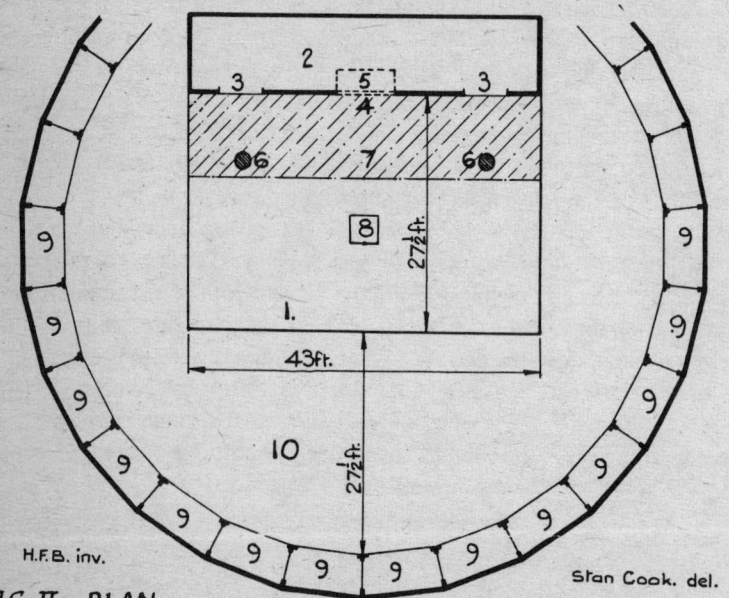

H.F.B. inv.   Stan Cook. del.

FIG II PLAN
1. Platform stage 2. Tiring-house 3. Tiring-house doors to stage 4. Conjectural third door 5. Conjectural discovery space (alternatively behind 3) 6. Pillars supporting the heavens 7. The heavens 8. Trap door 9. Spectators' gallery 10. The yard

The Globe

An artist's imaginative recreation of a typical Elizabethan theatre

FURTHER READING

Two good general surveys of Shakespeare's life and work as a playwright:

Reese, M. M., *Shakespeare, His World and his Work* (London: Arnold, 1980).

Speaight, Robert, *Shakespeare: The Man and his Achievement* (London: Dent, 1977).

Many of the themes and images introduced here are discussed at greater depth in the following books:

Price, Antony (ed.), *'A Midsummer Night's Dream' - Casebook* (London: Macmillan, 1983).

Barber, C. L., *Shakespeare's Festive Comedy*, Ch. 6 (Princeton: Princeton University Press, 1972).

Garber, Marjorie B., *Dreams in Shakespeare* (London: Yale University Press, 1974).

Watson, G. J., *Drama: an Introduction*, Ch. 5 (London: Macmillan, 1983).

Fender, S., *Shakespeare: 'A Midsummer Night's Dream'* (London: Arnold, 1968).

Young, David, *Something of Great Constancy, The Art of 'A Midsummer Night's Dream'* (London: Yale University Press, 1966).

Particularly useful discussions of Shakespeare's use of language and verse are to be found in the following:

Hulme, Hilda M., *Explorations in Shakespeare's Language* (London: Longmans, 1977).

Brooks, Harold (ed.), *The Arden Edition of Shakespeare's 'A Midsummer Night's Dream'* pp xxxiv-lvii (London: Methuen, 1979).

See also

Fender, S., *Shakespeare: 'A Midsummer Night's Dream'* (London: Arnold, 1968).

You will also find detailed help on the 'Speak the Speech' series of cassettes available from Sound News Studios, 18 Blenheim Road, London, W4.